A LIFETIME ADVENTURE

IF I SETTLE ON THE FAR SIDE OF THE SEA

DR. BRIAN THOMPSON

Invisible Inc. Publishing Company

Published by Invisible Inc. Publishing Company
2156 Walter Road, Westlake, Ohio 44145, USA
Dr. Brian Thompson 1.440.590.3440 / askbriant@gmail.com
Invisible Inc. Publishing Company is committed to helping people as they travel through the maze of life and preparing people for their eternal destiny. The Company expounds the belief expressed by the motto of the Great State of Ohio, "With God all things are possible."

Published in the United States of America
ISBN: 978-0-9705285-0-6
Biography & Autobiography / Personal Memoirs
15.12.10

DEDICATION

This book is dedicated to the hundreds, nay, thousands of people-family, friends, co-workers, pastors and others - who have had significant impact upon my life by their guidance, support, encouragement, companionship, comfort and in so many other ways.

Above all I dedicate this book to our wonderful Creator God without whom this book would have been impossible.

CONTENTS

1. First Memories 1
2. Meeting the Challenge 5
3. Family Life at 75 York Street 9
4. Early Rovings 13
5. Educational System 17
6. Reflections on the Early Years 19
7. Getting Better All the Time 23
8. The School in the Park 27
9. The Athletic Program at Thornes House 31
10. The Academic Program at Thornes House ... 35
11. Extracurricular Adventures 39
12. A Life Changing Experience 43
13. Summer Breaks 45
14. A Five Hundred Mile Hike 47
15. A Year of Transition 51
16. To the Far Side of the Sea 55
17. Life as a New Immigrant 59
18. Settling In 63
19. Pros and Cons 67
20. Romance at Seventeen 71
21. Marriage at Eighteen 75
22. A Place of New Beginnings 79
23. Settled In 83
24. Moving Forward 87
25. More Progress 91
26. On the Move Again 95
27. Reflections on Our Marriage 99
28. An Expanding Family 103

CONTENTS CONTINUED ON NEXT PAGE...

...CONTENTS CONTINUED

29. Five Steps Forward 107
30. More Steps Forward 111
31. Travel Adventures 115
32. Moving Along at North American 119
33. A Shift in Direction 123
34. A Big Challenge 127
35. Law School Notes 131
36. Horsefeathers 135
37. A Career Change 139
38. A Gathering Storm 143
39. Darkening Clouds 147
40. The Storm Hits 151
41. On the Road to Recovery 155
42. A Time of New Beginnings 159
43. A Wonderful Start 163
44. Happily Married 167
45. Active in Ministry 171
46. Facing Death Again 173
47. A Heart Wrenching Change 175
48. A Closer Walk 179
49. I Know Where I Am Going 183
50. Photos 185

1

First Memories

My earliest memory is that of my dad turning the couch upside down because planes were coming over dropping bombs. I was born in the year 1939, just a few months before the start of World War II. I was born in Europe, Northern England, in the city of Wakefield in West Yorkshire. I was number eight out of ten children, having seven sisters and two brothers. One sister and one brother were younger than I was. We lived on a housing estate which was owned by the local government and we were in a rented three bedroom house, semi-detached, with a small front flower garden and a larger vegetable garden in the back. How all twelve of us fitted into three bedrooms, I don't know, but I do remember when several of us had the chicken pox, we were all confined to one bedroom and laid sideways on the bed. But we did have an indoor bathroom with a bathtub, a small living/dining room and utility room, but no basement. But I'm sure that our vulnerability to enemy bombing attacks weighed heavily on the minds of my parents, Wilfred and Florence Thompson, and was partly responsible for the move to a much older row house near the heart of the city, at 75 York Street, a place where I would live until I was sixteen years old.

75 York Street provided our family with much needed space, with four decent sized bedrooms, a separate living room, a large kitchen and a full basement. In the basement was a large room, a coal storage area and best of all, a room with two metal pillars supporting corrugated sheeting which provided our own private shelter from the bombings. I don't believe that we would have survived a direct hit, but it provided a fair amount of protection and gave some sense of security. Our city of Wakefield was not hit by as many bombs as the more industrial cities nearby, like Leeds, but I remember the air raids well. We would just get to sleep when the air raid siren would sound, then my older sisters would wrap me in a blanket and take me into the basement "shelter". We would hear the planes flying over and eventually get the "all clear" siren and back to bed we would go.

My earliest memories are those of my dad and not of my mother. I remember going to the corner and sitting on the curb, waiting for him to come home from work. I remember him having part of the largest bedroom as a workshop and being in there with him. My dad was a "French Polisher" by trade. French polishing consisted of putting a special hand rubbed finish on wooden furniture. Then, when I was four years old, I remember a bed being placed in the living room and him laying in that bed day after day for several months. In our large kitchen, we had a huge table, with extra leaves in it. It sat twelve people. One night, we were all sitting around that table, waiting for word from the hospital. Then it came. My next memory is that of being in the living room. The curtains had been removed from the window. Whitewash had been applied to the window panes and I was lifted up to see my dad's body lying in the coffin there, his eyes still wide open.

As I was growing up I was told that my dad had died from a nervous breakdown, and that may have been part of it. Later in life I learned the true story. My dad had served in the army in World War I, but by the time World War II started, he was a pacifist. The enemy was dropping bombs on us and he was taking the position that we should not resist. This did not set well with his fellow workers and they gave him a severe beating from which he eventually died.

And so my mother was faced with a tremendous challenge. My younger brother had died in infancy from pneumonia, so she had nine children to raise, the oldest still being a teenager. It was 1943. The war was still going on. The enemy had overrun almost all of Europe. Food was scarce. How would the family survive?

2

MEETING THE CHALLENGE

My mother was a truly remarkable woman. Her name was Florence Deborah Thompson but her maiden name was Salt. She told us that she went to school with a lad named Pepper. Friends and family called her "Flo." We called her "Mam." When she was 87 years old she started writing the memories of her life and completed the writing when she was 89. In mother's memories she tells how she was the sixth of twelve children. She left school at age 13 and got her first job wheeling and unloading tile and bricks at a brick works, working from six o'clock in the morning until five o'clock in the late afternoon, Mondays through Fridays, and on Saturday from six until twelve o'clock noon. Then she worked in a munitions factory wheeling heavy shells for the last part of World War I. So my mother was used to hard work and facing challenges.

But how would the family survive, with the oldest yet a teenager and the youngest being seven months old, nine children and one mother? Mother was entitled to a small widow's pension, which she accepted. She probably would have been able to collect welfare but it was contrary to her values and work ethic. So mother went out to work as a cleaning lady, six o'clock until nine o'clock in the morning and six until nine in the evening to provide money for food, rent, electricity and coal. She prepared our big cooked meal at noon each weekday, emptied the chamber pots and washed all of the clothes and bedding and mostly prepared afternoon tea. The older children took care of the younger children and we all had lots of chores to do. My usual chores as I was growing up were the following: washing dishes, scrubbing the linoleum on the kitchen floor on my hands and knees, scrubbing the front outdoor steps and rubbing soft yellow stone on the edges to make it attractive, and bringing up buckets of coal from the basement/cellar. THE STRATEGY WORKED. WE ALL PULLED TOGETHER. WE NOT ONLY SURVIVED BUT WE THRIVED.

Those years of wheeling bricks and munitions had given my mother unusual physical strength, preparing her for the task ahead. For example, this is how she washed clothes. First, she had to boil water. The "boiler" in the basement was a hollowed out gigantic stone with a coal fire underneath it. Water had to be ladled into it, then ladled out when hot. Next, the washing "machine" had a large handle attached to it to turn the agitator. Mother was the motor! Then the wringer was operated by manually turning the handle. Finally, the clothes and bedding were taken outside to be pegged to the clothes line. If it started to rain, they would have to be brought back inside until the rain stopped. Sometimes it would rain black soot from the many coal fires in the neighborhood.

But in spite of all of the hard work, mother had some enjoyable moments. After getting home from work at 9:00 a.m., she would fix herself a big mug of tea, sit in her favorite chair, listen to the radio, including her favorite program, "Five to Ten" and then doze off for a while before cooking the midday meal. Sometimes she would sing along with the radio - songs like, "The Old Rugged Cross," and, "The New Jerusalem." In the evening, at 9:00 p.m., she would walk home with her work friend, Mrs. Kershaw, and they would stop and talk outside the front of the house for a long time before mother would come in.

Mother lived to be 93 years old. All the years that I was privileged to have her, she would say, "I have my memories," reflecting on a life well lived. At the end of her written memories she writes, "It's been very hard work, but it's been worth it."

3

FAMILY LIFE AT 75 YORK STREET

Growing up with seven sisters and one remaining brother was a wonderful experience. We were very poor, but we didn't think much about it because everyone around us was poor - no cars, no telephones, no labor saving devices. Food was rationed and we had coupon books so we could buy sugar, tea, and other basics. But we had a loving, caring, family relationship. Yes, we had a few very minor disagreements, but they were very far between. Like ones between me and my younger sister. The two of us were assigned the task of washing and drying dishes, which was a big chore in such a large family, so we would disagree as to who would wash and who would wipe with the tea towel.

Without TV, computers, cell phones etc. there was plenty of time for table games such as snakes and ladders, monopoly and dominoes, all of which we enjoyed immensely. We had a radio that we listened to from time to time. Listening to plays and other programs caused me to imagine the visual characteristics which expanded my imagination. When company came, which was very frequent, we would start up the gramophone and play records. Every now and then the gramophone would slow down and I would wind it up again. We also had some outdoor games. Very few people had cars, so a half hour or an hour would go by before a car came up or down the street. We would chalk out some squares on the road, write numbers in the squares and play hopscotch.

And many of my sisters loved to bake, making everything from the very basic ingredients. Of course I was allowed to help and I especially enjoyed licking out any remaining batter from the mixing bowls. Besides baking, many were good cooks. I believe Violet's specialty was Yorkshire Pudding which was somewhat like pancake but was risen, baked in the oven and served with gravy, mashed potatoes, meat and fresh vegetable. All of this was without recipe books, just hand me down information, a pinch of this and a dash of that. And we were without any real temperature controls. A coal fire was used for heat and for cooking, baking and garbage disposal. We did have a hot plate with a broiler underneath it and an electric tea kettle which was constantly in use, but we almost always used the fire since it was needed for heat and didn't cost any more to place a pan on the grating in front. The oven was heated by opening a damper so that heat from the fire would go under and around it. So the oven temperature was unpredictable and sometimes cakes would sag in the middle, but overall we got by quite well.

Our food was really quite simple. Breakfast was toast and tea, just that. Slices of white bread were buttered on one side, with the other side toasted over the fire, so it had a special flavor from the burning coal. Mother said that we could afford cereal, but we couldn't afford the milk that was needed to help it go down. At school we each were given a small bottle of milk during morning play time. School meals were available, but we didn't like what was offered, things like pureed peas, so we went home at midday and our loving mother would provide our big cooked meal of the day: mashed potatoes, cabbage or cauliflower, etc., a small sliver of roast beef, rice or bread pudding and often some specialty of her own. Nothing was wasted. If it was not eaten at one meal, it was waiting at the next. Then came tea time. We had to eat everything with bread, to make it go further. First a salad with lettuce, sliced hard boiled egg, sliced radishes and maybe some mayonnaise. Then half a canned peach in syrup with canned condensed milk and bread and butter. Finally, maybe some homemade cake or tarts. For bed-time snack back to toast. As a growing, active boy, I was always hungry, but there was always bread, butter and jam or bread with pan drippings (from roasting meat) and HP sauce (like Worcestershire sauce) available to me, but I had to make sure that I was hungry enough at meal times to eat the entire meal.

As time went on, my older sisters attended local social activities, such as the dance hall and roller rink where young women met young men and relationships were formed. Our family expanded to add brothers in law, with a wedding taking place about every two years. After the ceremony, the reception would take place at our house. Family and guests would take turns eating, seated twelve at a time around our large kitchen table, with several seatings taking place. Due to the war, housing was scarce. So the newlyweds would live with us for a few years and were given a bedroom of their own. After a while someone would run down the street to the red telephone booth and the midwife would be called. Then water would be boiled after which came a baby's cry - a miracle of birth had taken place.

4

EARLY ROVINGS

E ven in those early years, I had a strong sense that my mother trusted me. She allowed me great freedom to roam around town, exploring and observing and finding my own entertainment and expanding my horizons. My earliest entertainment was found by going a few blocks to the local slaughter house, standing by the entrance and watching the sheep being slaughtered. Often I would get chased away, but soon I would be back. My brother Arthur took a job as a projectionist at one of the local movie theaters. So all I had to do was show up there and say, "Arthur sent me," and the lady with the flashlight would show me to my seat. Sometimes they would question it and check with "Arthur," but I was always allowed in. My brother's boss was also named Arthur, so I believed that helped too. Mostly I watched Westerns - Cowboys and Indians - which showed scenery of an amazing place on the far side of the sea. Then I had aunts and uncles to visit who lived within three miles of our house. I loved to read, and one of my favorite newspaper cartoons was that of a boy who would travel through distant lands all in one day but would always be back home for afternoon tea and calmly say to his mother, "What's for tea mam!"

Early on, I wanted to be a medical doctor. I would carry scissors and first aid supplies in my pocket in case there was an accident. I would not have known what to do if there had been an accident, but I wanted to help in any way I could. I remember borrowing a book or books from the local library about Biology so I could start preparing. When I was eight or nine years old, I started my own small business. My hometown of Wakefield had a large farmers' market every Saturday. People came from surrounding areas to shop. At the end of market day, I would pick up wooden orange crates and other boxes, take them home, chop them up and make small bundles of firewood. Then I would go door to door selling them for three pence each so people could start their coal fires.

I developed a love of nature and of gardening. We lived in a row house and the back yard was mostly asphalt with some concrete. Before he died, my dad had placed a border of bricks around part of the yard, then filled it in with about four inches of soil. That became my very first garden. One of my favorite flowering plants was Virginia Stock along with Snapdragons and Alyssum, and I planted some vegetables. The soil was not very fertile. There was little sunlight. But I enjoyed my little garden.

And I developed friendships with several boys I went to school with. It was a custom in that place and at that time, at Christmas, for young boys to go in small groups, door to door, and sing some Christmas carols. So we would join in doing that. We would sing a few carols, knock on the door and be given a few small coins. Sometimes we would be invited inside for a cup of tea and a biscuit (cookie).

My special friend, Brian Jeffries and I were especially close. We spent hours and hours outside in the summers playing cricket. It was a slow game, and I don't remember the rules now, but we enjoyed it immensely. And, of course, we kicked a small ball around, like the beginnings of soccer. I spent a lot of time at Brian's house playing table games and just visiting. Brian had an older brother, Frank, who was sports editor for the local newspaper. He had a mother and dad who were both really friendly to me. Brian's dad was a lay minister with John Street Congregational Church and Brian attended the Sunday afternoon Sunday school there.

When I was eleven years old Brian invited me to Sunday school, so I went, and John Street became my church from then on. I remember us building a little club house just beyond the back of his house using loose bricks and loose asbestos roofing from a school construction project there. Brian Jeffries passed the eleven plus exam as I did, and was scheduled to attend the same high school/grammar school so it looked as if our good relationship would continue. But all that was to change because of the educational system at that time.

5

EDUCATIONAL SYSTEM

Our next door neighbors on one side were unruly to say the least. Later on, the dad of the house reportedly was hit over the head with a poker by his daughter, and needed hospitalization and stitches. Because my mother did not want me to be influenced by their swearing, she started me into school at age four. That first year of school we had some instruction in the morning, learning personal hygiene - brushing teeth with a hard toothpaste, etc., and learning basic alphabet and numbers. Then in the afternoon we slept in cots, although I would just lie there with my eyes wide open.

In first grade, I remember having a really good teacher, which was the only good overall teacher I had until age eleven. We had morning and afternoon playtime in the school yard. I was the only boy wearing wooden shoes so I was in command, threatening to kick with them. The boys and the girls had separate playgrounds.

After that, the teachers may have been effective at teaching, but they were mean. They kept a bamboo cane hidden up the chimney so the school inspectors wouldn't see it and they would discipline us by having us hold out our hand then, "WHACK" - that really stung! One teacher, Mrs. Smith, thought she heard someone talking in class but didn't know who it was. So she had all of us line up and "WHACK" to each one. Miss Elvidge caned me so hard that I told my mother, who went right to the school and threatened to report her. Soon after that Miss Elvidge moved to Australia. Miss Elvidge was an effective teacher of math though. We recited math tables over and over again so that, even now, if I need the answer to a multiplication question, its right there. Until age eleven, all of us boys wore short pants, and teacher Mr. Brown would have one of us stand at his desk for a prolonged period of time, talking while he put his hand up the boy's pants leg.

Then it was time to take the eleven plus exam. Those who did really well on the exam would have the privilege of attending high school, which was sometimes called grammar school. Those who did not do as well would attend secondary modern school, learn some trades and finish school at age fourteen or fifteen. Those who did not do well on the eleven plus exam would have a second chance by taking another exam a year or two later and then, if they did extremely well, would transition into high school, but few did. Thankfully, I passed the eleven plus exam, making wide opportunities available to me.

One very positive aspect of those early years in school was that we started each day with an assembly of the entire school body where we sang a hymn, had a Bible reading and said a prayer - including the Lord's Prayer - which we all recited together. One hymn has stayed with me down through the years, "All things bright and beautiful, all creatures great and small, all things wise and wonderful, The Lord God made them all." One funny hymn we all loved began with these words, "A cuckoo flew out of the woods to say, 'Cuckoo'." And a somewhat political one talked about, "These dark satanic mills." Then we had some religious instruction during class time, memorizing Biblical passages such as the story of the good Samaritan, which was given to illustrate that we are to love our neighbor as ourself.

6

REFLECTIONS ON THE EARLY YEARS

A s I reflect on those first eleven years of my life, I think of the people, events and circumstances that had a tremendous effect on the development of my character and personality that are a part of who I am even today. There were both positive and negative influences. The negatives I had to deal with well into my adult life. Thankfully, the positive aspects were very strong and have helped me throughout my life.

The biggest influence, as you may have surmised, was that of my mother. Her influence was not so much by what she said, although that was quite significant, but by her tremendous example in the face of the most trying of circumstances. Her example of hard work, a sense of duty, her loving care of all of us, her honesty and integrity was passed on to all of us from the very beginning. I always had the sense that Mother completely trusted me as she allowed me to roam and explore the places beyond our home. I always felt I could talk to her about anything that was bothering me and she would understand. One time, at age eleven, I felt I needed to sit on my mother's lap. My sisters were deriding me, but she let me. So I sat on her lap for a while, felt satisfied and went away completely at ease.

My mother never took me to church, but when she was growing up she was in church on Sunday mornings, afternoons and evenings and on Tuesday evenings, so she was ingrained with Biblical values. She would often say to me, "Do unto others as you would have them do to you," and she followed that as one of the guiding principles in her life, taking in family members, friends and even strangers. But I didn't find out where that saying of hers came from until I was an adult. Another saying of my mother's, which has been a primary guiding principle throughout my life is, "That's main." To follow the most important things in life, to find the most important thing in any situation and have done with lesser things, simplifies life and brings focus and success. I can still hear in my mind my mother talking: Entering a house, it's "wipe your feet," sitting on a chair, it's "that chair has four legs." Mother did provide this little lad with some entertainment though. I was amazed that my mother could take her teeth out. So when company came I would want them to also see this feat, and Mother would reluctantly comply with my request.

My mother taught me an extremely valuable lesson - not to manipulate people. A friend of mine was having a birthday party, but I was not invited. So I devised a scheme: I would take one of my prized possessions, go to his house, offer it as a birthday gift and they would invite me in. So I did that, and it worked. I happily ran back and told my mother. My mother recognized my deception and firmly said, "NO!" I learned a lesson. No birthday party and a prized possession gone.

Even though we were very poor, my mother was able to expand our horizons by taking us on walks in the country, to concerts of the Yorkshire Symphony Orchestra and on visits with family and friends. She provided for us to take piano lessons. If we had tomatoes they would be the best quality tomatoes. There was always a bowl of fruit available, and we were allowed to have one fresh fruit per day. She even gave us an allowance each week. Mine was three pence - just enough to go to the sweet shop (candy store) a block away and stand in front of the window trying to decide what to get this week.

It was wonderful growing up in a loving family, where we all pulled in the same direction. We all grew close to one another. It was always, "OUR Brian" and "OUR Ethel," spoken with tenderness and affection. We had met the challenges and overcome them, and this gave us a feeling of exuberance and accomplishment, helping us to face future challenges with confidence. And the whole community showed that same spirit. The war had brought us together in a fellowship of suffering, with many a loved one lost because of the war. There was a big celebration as the war ended, with dancing in the streets and a huge bonfire in the center of town with an effigy of the enemy hanging in the flames. A stranger man lifted me onto his shoulders so I could see it clearly. Despite British reserve and reluctance to impose, the clerks in the stores, the bank tellers and all would add the word "Love" to each and every greeting. It was, "What would you like, Love?" and "Thank you, Love."

But the war had left me with anxiety, a sense of impending doom. And the oppression of my early school teachers had left me with some distrust of those in authority. I don't remember whether it was my mother or my sisters who would tell me when I misbehaved, "Bobby will get you," but I know that I developed a fear of the police. The reality was that the police were kind and gentle and did not carry guns. Every evening the Bobby would walk down my street checking all the doors and knocking on any door he found unlocked to remind the residents there to lock their doors for the night. And who would we ask for directions? - the local Bobby.

And there was always a void in my life from growing up without a dad. I treasured relationships with uncles, especially my Uncle Jack who lived alone. If I had wind that he might be coming to visit, I would go to the bus station and wait for hours hoping to not miss a minute of time with him. But he very rarely actually came.

Then there was a negative aspect of growing up in a female dominated family, with my mother, seven sisters and one brother. I could relate much more easily to women than to men.

At age eleven, then, I was ready for the next five years of great adventure and expanded horizons as my life in England continued.

7

GETTING BETTER ALL THE TIME

The year when I turned age eleven was a pivotal year in my life. After that time everything got better at 75 York Street. My sisters were getting married, lived with us for a while, then moved into new housing built and rented out by the local government. This eased a lot of the strain on the family budget. Also, my older brother, Arthur, only sixteen years old, got a job with the railroad working on the steam locomotives. The locomotives were powered by steam produced in a huge boiler heated by a continually fed coal fire. Arthur's job was to shovel coal from the tender into the fire. It was extremely hard work, but Arthur built up tremendous strength in his arms and upper body and earned good wages and was able to help provide support for the family.

I was able to do my part by working part time. For some time I had an early morning newspaper route. The customers were spread out across town, so I would run the entire three miles each morning, delivering.

Then, as the family expanded, I would babysit for my sisters. And my love of gardening increased more and more. Just digging gave me a lot of pleasure and satisfaction. Being now in new housing, my sisters and brothers-in-law needed much help in breaking up the hard ground, planting a tiny lawn and flowers and bushes in front and a vegetable garden in back. My uncles, too, were getting older and needed help with their landscaping and gardens. So after school I would often walk a few miles to one of their houses, visit, enjoy a meal, do some work and walk back home. It seems that every vegetable garden had a rhubarb patch in it. At the evening meal we often had a dish of stewed rhubarb, sweetened, with custard on top - delicious! I often think of my home town, Wakefield, as being in rhubarb country, because whole fields filled with rows of rhubarb plants surrounded the city.

One thing that my uncles' and sisters' gardens needed was fertilizer. In that place and at that time horses would still go up and down the streets pulling wagons. So there was plenty of free fertilizer just laying there. I got two big wooden chests that had contained tea shipped from Ceylon, fastened them to a set of wheels and frame from a baby carriage, and went about town collecting horse manure. Sometimes people would wonder what was in the chests, peek inside and then turn away in disgust.

As the family rapidly expanded in number and spread out but remained closely knit, there was a need for us all to get together. None of us had telephones and none of us had vehicles, but Wakefield was a market town and our house was close to the market and shopping at the center of town. So a tradition was started by which everyone would come in on a Saturday, market day, do shopping and we would all have lunch together. By then we were able to afford fish and chips from the fish and chips shop which was only fifty yards away through our back yard. The fish were fresh and delicious. They were caught in the North Sea which was about sixty miles away and shipped to our town the same morning. Before that time we had only been able to afford fish cakes and chips (fries). Fish cakes were slices of potato with a little bit of fish in between and dipped in batter then fried.

We were now able to take a bath at the local slipper baths where we could rent a bathtub with hot and cold running water, rent a clean towel and buy a small sliver of soap. Often I would overstay my time in the tub and the ladies in charge would bang loudly on my door and remind me. Prior to that time all we had were two zinc tubs in the basement with the need to heat water in the hollowed-out stone over the coal fire and ladle the water in and out of the tub.

Not having a bathroom in the house presented challenges. Across the yard there was a row of flush toilets, one for each house, but these would sometimes freeze up in winter. When it was dark outside, my sisters would want me to go with them and stand at the end of the row while they did their business. If we were alone, and we ran out of paper (only could afford newspaper) we would keep yelling, "paper!" hoping that someone would hear us.

Having had financial difficulties early on, the electric company had put us on a "pay as you go" method. Sometimes our lights would suddenly go out and someone would have to go into the basement with a flashlight and put a coin, a shilling, in the meter.

There were special times when we all got together. One time, one of my brothers-in-law rented a bus and driver for a day. We went all over town, picking up family, and then went to the seaside for an enjoyable outing. Then, of course, Christmas and Easter were special times. I thoroughly enjoyed all of my nephews and nieces. I know that eventually I had at least twenty one of them. My sister Deborah had a son, Mark who lived with us. I wheeled Mark all over town in his perambulator (pram, baby carriage) and later he became my godson as well as my nephew.

At the same time as all of this, I was experiencing great adventures which I will relate in the next few chapters.

8

THE SCHOOL
IN THE PARK

Having passed the eleven plus exam, I had the distinct privilege of attending high school. In my hometown there were three high schools. There were an all girls high school and an all boys high school which seemed to be for students from higher class families and wealthy families, with those who had not passed the eleven plus exam being able to pay tuition in order to attend. I was assigned to the third high school which was named Thornes House Grammar School which was attended by students who were commoners. My mother had always impressed on me that we were common folk and not entitled to all that was available to upper class people.

Thornes House turned out to be a tremendous blessing in my life. I had developed a great love of the outdoors and the school helped to satisfy my desire to be close to nature. Thornes House was a big converted mansion located in the middle of a big park that was adjacent to two other big parks. To the mansion there had been added a new wing which provided additional classrooms. But the old part had classrooms with French Windows which opened up to a gigantic rose garden with a large fountain. After I had attended for a year, during summer break (six weeks) my brother Arthur came running into our house and told us the news, "'Forns 'owse bun't dahn t't grahnd.." So we all went to see what had happened. We found that the old part of the school had been totally consumed by the fire but that the new wing was intact. So how would we be able to continue having regular classes? There was a big mansion in the next adjoining park that was taken over to replace the classroom space. That mansion had a big rock garden with many interesting plants and flowers and had a very long driveway lined with gigantic horse chestnut trees. So break time was increased and we continually had enjoyable walks through the park going from one building to the other. Very close to Thornes House there was an extensive public rose garden and flower garden with a pond on which water lilies gracefully sat. Near the other mansion there was a steep hill at the top of which was a terrific view - we could see for more than five miles in the distance.

Thornes House was a mile and half from our home. I went home in the middle of the day to enjoy the delicious meal that my mother had prepared. I had an hour and a half for lunch so I had just enough time to walk home, eat the big meal she had prepared and talk with her, then walk back in time for the afternoon sessions. But going to and from school, six miles a day, was enjoyable. My next older sister, Olive, had also passed the eleven plus exam and was at Thornes House with me for two or three years. So we would often walk together and talk on the way. She taught me some rules as we walked and talked, such as "the man needs to walk on the outside of the sidewalk, next to the gutter, so that if a car or carriage comes along and muddy water splashes up, the man gets drenched but the woman stays dry." Often I would walk to or from school with classmates and we would talk along the way. I remember one such friend who had homing pigeons. He would have some pigeons in his jacket. When we would get near the school he would release them and they would fly back to their roost. Often we would play "conkers" on the way to and from school and at break times. There were many horse chestnut trees in the area that produced a fruit/nut similar to our Ohio buckeye. We would drill a hole through the middle of the "conker," put it on string, then take turns hitting the opponent's conker. The owner of the conker which survived was the winner. An advantage could be gained by keeping a conker for a year or two until it was good and hard.

Unlike the other two high schools, Thornes House was a mixed gender school. The boys would go in one entrance and the girls would go in another, but we would meet together in class.

I only know of two romances that developed in our class in all of my years at Thornes House. But I believe it was good for me to be in class with both girls and boys and have some interaction with both. We all wore school uniforms. The boys wore a navy blue blazer, white shirt, yellow and blue striped tie, gray pants and a cap. The symbol of the Thornes family was the stork. So we had a badge crest with a stork on our caps and on the pocket of our blazer. The uniform helped keep us out of trouble, because, if we misbehaved, people could tell readily which school to come to to find us. The girls wore a white blouse with a yellow and blue striped tie, a beret with a stork badge on it a jumper, white socks and black shoes. Having school uniforms helped keep us from trying to outdo one another and helped to promote equality and unity. I do confess though, that I broke with tradition somewhat. Instead of getting my clothes for me, my mother started giving me a clothing allowance. So I went to the store and found a pair of green gabardine pants that I liked that were at a lower price. The other boys were wearing gray pants, but my independent spirit had me wearing green. I was questioned about it, but I prevailed for a while.

In the next chapter we will continue with the Thornes House experience.

9

THE ATHLETIC PROGRAM AT THORNES HOUSE

Being full of energy at that age, Thornes House satisfied our need for physical exertion.

A separate building housed a large gymnasium, wood shop, metal shop and an assembly hall big enough to seat the entire student body of five hundred. The gymnasium had climbing bars all around and was fully equipped. There was a boys entrance at one end and a girls entrance at the other, each with a locker room and shower. We enjoyed an hour of physical training two mornings each week doing all kinds of exercise and then took a shower. Our teacher, Mr. Rennie, seemed to be in his mid or later forties but he was quite spry and did all the exercises with us. He would line us up by the shower afterwards, allow each of us a few seconds to shower (rinse off) and blow his whistle when it was time for the next one to step up. Sometimes we would do our physical training outside - the long jump, the high jump or track. Sometimes we would run seven miles or so cross country - out of the parks, along the canal, along the roads and back. When I would run the mile I would hold back most of the way, then put on a big burst of speed at the end, amazing everyone. So I was good at cross country, the endurance test. When I was training for cross country, I would get up early in the morning and run three to five miles before breakfast.

Besides having physical training two mornings each week, we also had an afternoon each week for sports, which I loved. My home town of Wakefield had a rugby football team named Wakefield Trinity. Rugby football is a fast moving contact sport with an amazing flying tackle. Most of the players were local coal miners, with tremendous upper body strength. But it was a dangerous sport, played without shoulder pads or helmets, and broken legs were a common occurrence. I attended most of the home games of Wakefield Trinity and most of the away games, always in the less expensive "standing only" section. So the safe game we boys mostly played at Thornes House was soccer. We played when it was snowing. We played when it was raining. We enjoyed every minute of it. I played right wing, running the whole length of the field; back and forth, back and forth. In warmer weather, we boys played cricket which was a slow, relaxing game. Professional teams would take days to play one game, but we could fit a game into one afternoon. The girls at Thornes House played field hockey for part of the year and netball the rest of the year. Netball was the equivalent of our basketball.

So attending Thornes House was a distinct privilege. I often wonder how I did so well to not only pass the eleven plus exam but to also do so well on it. I got the impression that I had attended a substandard elementary school. For instance, in the elementary school we were only taught to print and did not learn cursive handwriting. When I started at Thornes House I was told that I should already have learned cursive handwriting. So I had to teach myself, but even today my writing is part printing and part cursive. I was always an avid reader though. When I was little my sisters would put me to bed at eight p.m. then keep checking to make sure I was asleep. But I would have my head under the covers, reading with a flashlight. And we had newspapers delivered daily which I read from front to back. After we read the newspapers, they were put to good use. Some were used along with kindling wood to start the coal fires. Some were taken to the local fish and chips shop to wrap the food in. Some were used for personal hygiene (we could not afford bathroom tissue). So I believe that all of my reading, all that my older siblings taught me, the learning of math tables by rote, and what I learned from having the freedom to explore the places outside our home, gave me the advantage I needed to do well on the eleven plus exam.

Needless to say, with all of the physical activity; physical training, sports, walking six miles a day going to and from school, working in my sister's and uncle's gardens, etc., I slept very soundly and had a very good appetite and built up good physical strength.

10

THE ACADEMIC PROGRAM AT THORNES HOUSE

For almost all of us students, we were on a five year program, from age eleven to age sixteen, culminating in the taking of exams from which we earned the general certificate of education - ordinary level for those subjects in which we had a passing grade. We began with some basic subjects, then concentrated on seven subjects, some required, some elected, on which we would take the exam. A very few students would stay for two additional years, then take an exam to gain the general certificate of education - advanced level. Only these few students would have the opportunity to attend college.

As new students, we were divided into three classes of about thirty five students in each class. The students who had done the best on the eleven plus exam were assigned to one class and students were assigned to the other two classes based on how well they had performed on the eleven plus. I was assigned to the class of the highest achievers and my long time friend, Brian Jeffries was assigned to one of the lower classes. Very disappointingly to me, from that point on our relationship changed. We were still friends but our relationship just was not the same. One blessing for me, though, was that our regular classroom was in the corner of the building with windows on two walls. Although my back was to the rose garden, I was seated near the front by the wall across from the side window, so I could look at the teacher and out the window at the same time. The side window looked out onto a grove of beech trees and in the autumn I would pick up beech nuts and have them on my desk to munch whenever the teacher looked the other way.

The academic program at Thornes House was excellent. The teachers were excellent. The teachers treated us students with complete respect. We treated the teachers with complete respect. At the beginning of class, when the teacher came into the room, we would all stand at attention until the teacher was all the way in and sat down. When our French teacher came in, (I had five years of French) while we were standing, she would say, "Bonjour, mes élèves," then we would say together, "Bonjour, mademoiselle," then she would say, "Asseyez vous" (Sit down). We had no fear of physical punishment from any of the teachers. The only person in the whole school who was allowed to give corporal punishment was the headmaster, Mr. Bracewell, who could hit a student on the buttocks with a slipper if ever needed. There were a few prefects with authority to give the punishment of detention for minor infractions of the rules. Prefects were chosen from among the advanced group of students in the sixteen to eighteen age range. I only remember having one detention - for being late to school one day. Detention meant that we would be kept an extra hour on Friday after regular classes. We would be together in a classroom with a prefect watching over us while we wrote, over and over, such things as, "I will not be late for school."

Each student received a progress report three times a year which had to be signed by a parent and each student took exams in each subject once a year. I started out weak in English and some other subjects but rapidly improved, except for art class. My art teacher wrote on my report card, "tries, but has some difficulty with drawing." But there was something I could do well in art class. I could sit still, so one time I was chosen to sit in front facing my classmates while they drew a picture of me. One subject I started out strong on and stayed strong on throughout was mathematics. I loved algebra, geometry, logarithms and trigonometry and my math teacher, Mr. Glick was superb. In English literature we memorized passages from Milton and Shakespeare, which I can still quote today. In French we repeated verb forms over and over and I can still rattle those off. Physics, chemistry, and history I did fairly well in. I took the ordinary level exam in seven subjects and passed in five of them. The big disappointment to me was that I failed geography, because I loved geography. Geography took me to places far away, lands on the far side of the sea. I distinctly remember sitting in geography class and learning about a country called the United States of America, with the Great Lakes and ore boats traveling from Duluth, Minnesota to Cleveland, Ohio, not realizing how significant that would be to me.

One thing that stands out as being lacking in the academic program at Thornes House was communication skills, especially speaking. There was a debating club which met after class time, but I was reserved, somewhat an introvert and somewhat timid that way, so I did not participate. Then there was the matter of cultural language, which was tied up in class distinction. The local way of speaking was called "Broad Yorkshire." However, my mother was from Staffordshire. My manner of speaking was partly that of Staffordshire, also, the teachers at Thornes House said that we had to speak "Oxford English" which was the manner of speaking of people of the upper most class of society. So with my mixed way of speaking I was extremely self-conscious and hesitant to speak.

But overall, life at Thornes House was wonderful. We had some homework but it was not overwhelming. I had time to join the choir and we would travel to churches, etc. to perform. And I had time for the amazing travel adventures that I will relate, starting in the next chapter.

11

EXTRACURRICULAR ADVENTURES

Mabel was one of my cousins. She was twenty five years old and single, and I was eleven when she offered to take me on a one week adventure by the sea. We would join the Youth Hostels Association then go hiking along the East Coast of Yorkshire, walking about ten miles each day and staying at Youth Hostels along the way. I readily accepted and my mother approved. And so began a series of new adventures that gave me another outlet for my high energy levels. That initial trip was wonderful. Youth Hostels were places where we could stay for a night and pay just a nominal fee. We could do our own cooking or pay extra for supper and breakfast. The Hostels were closed in the day time. To qualify to stay we had to be traveling "under our own steam" which meant as hikers or cyclists. Each person had to bring a sleeping "bag" which was just made of a thin cotton sheet. Blankets and army style bunk beds were provided. There was a men's dormitory and a women's dormitory. The Hostels were various style buildings that had been donated to or acquired by the organization. Some were converted farm houses, smaller mansions, small schools, etc. On that first trip we leisurely walked along the public footpath that went all along the top of the cliffs overlooking the North Sea. We stayed in resort towns and villages beginning with Bridlington, then Filey, Scarborough, Robin Hoods Bay and Whitby.

Mabel and I also joined the local Youth Hostels Association. Besides having regular meetings, the local group would go hosteling on weekends. For us, this usually meant leaving town after the work week ended at noon on Saturday, taking the bus to a place close to a Hostel, hiking to the Hostel, staying for the night, then going on a twenty to twenty five mile hike on Sunday. Often this was a hike over the hills and dales of Yorkshire or across the moors. The moors were miles and miles of reservation land held in a public trust and were covered with heather and a few patches of grass here and there. A number of sheep wandered around and bleated as we traveled the many trails.

The Youth Hostel at Filey, a small village on the east coast of Yorkshire, had a special program for a week at Christmas time. So Mabel and I went and joined in all the activities. One activity I remember clearly was an all day treasure hunt throughout the village, on the beach, in the little church, etc., following clues, then an exchange of results at dinner in the evening. We did not do any real hiking that week but we had a truly relaxing time and developed friendships.

After a couple of years of Youth Hosteling though, Mabel's interests turned elsewhere. She met Tony, a school teacher, who she eventually married. However, I was thirteen years old and my mother gave me the freedom to continue hosteling without Mabel. Had she known what I would undertake one weekend with the local group, though, she might have pulled in the reins for a while. I wrote about that special weekend for the school magazine at Thornes House:

"An attempt at Potholing"
A bracing wind and the clamour of curlews and lapwings greeted us at half past nine one autumn morning as we climbed out of the valley, leaving Pateley

Bridge Youth Hostel behind us. There was a large party, sixteen in number, led by the Hostel Warden. We soon struck the old road which crosses the high moors from Grassington to Pateley Bridge, and passing through Greenhow, we came in sight of the cavern entrance which we reached at ten o'clock.

Once there, we deposited our rucksacks in the cabin, had a cup of tea and made ready for the descent. We passed through the part of the cavern system known as the "Show Cave," reached by a sloping stairway forty-to-fifty feet deep. At last, with helmets to protect us from sharp overhead rocks and torches lit, we turned into a side passage and started to descend in earnest. The passage grew smaller; we had to slide down chutes with sharp rocks sticking into our backs and sides. A stream had once flowed through the passage and deposited a deep bed of silt through which a narrow channel had been dug. Deep pools of mud and water had collected in the channel and my feet were soon wet through. By now we could not stand upright. We crawled, backs bent double, through seemingly unending masses of mud. Every half-hour we had a short rest, when we checked the number present. The passage became narrower still, and I saw in front of me the shoulder of a hanging mass of rock beneath which was a pool of water. As the rock was so low, I had to plunge into the water, moving on my elbows and knees but just managing to keep my body clear of the surface of the pool.

After what seemed hours of crawling, when sometimes it was stuffy, sometimes it was cold; when my torch went out after being under water too many times; when we took the wrong turning and had to retrace our steps; we at last reached a perpendicular cleft in the rock, a chimney, at the foot of which ran a stream. This chimney was twenty feet high and to ascend each person had to push against one side with his hands and feet and press his back against the opposite side. My legs and arms were not long enough. Nor were those of some other members of the party. Those who could not climb up were told that the others would not be more than half-an-hour and were left with a candle.

Soon the noise made by the climbers died away. We waited and waited. The cold nipped our wet hands and feet. The others waiting grew tired of doing nothing there in the cold and gloom. They decided to return to the entrance without the guide. Knowing how easy it was to get lost, I did not go with

41

them but stayed there alone. I waited and waited. The candle got shorter and shorter. I grew colder and colder and the noise of the stream began to play on my nerves. I kept jumping up, imagining that I heard noises coming from the chimney but nobody came. At last, I did hear voices, speaking real words calling from the chimney. I went forward and helped people down, learning from them the cause of the delay. Several of the party had descended a ten foot drop into a cave known as the "Rat Trap." Each had helped the other out until it came to the turn of the last man. It had taken well over an hour to haul him out by means of a series of belts tied together.

We then started off back, on the two mile crawl to the entrance. After another hard struggle through the narrow muddy passages, twelve exhausted, mud-plastered, slouching bodies emerged into the dazzling sunlight and flung themselves onto the grass. It was then four o'clock in the afternoon and we had been underground for nearly six hours.

B. Thompson

12

A LIFE CHANGING EXPERIENCE

And so then while yet thirteen years old, almost fourteen, I started going Youth Hosteling alone, no Mabel and no local club members. I say "alone" but I did not feel alone. As I hiked over the moors, the hills and across fields in the dales, I was meditating; processing deep thoughts about life, about my place in it, about the futility of war and strife, about the scripture passages I had memorized in school, and so on. And as I meditated and pondered, I sensed that answers were being given to me. One such experience I have published several times in local newspapers as a Good Friday message: *"WHY IS GOOD FRIDAY CALLED GOOD?*

I was walking through a field near Otley, in northern England. It was on a Good Friday and I was pondering over the question, "Why is Good Friday called good?". At the beginning of each school day the headmaster read some words from the Good News book, so I had heard that on the first Good Friday a man was executed and because of his execution we could come to a place of new beginning in our lives. For the God-man who was executed was the Creator of the world, Jesus the Christ, who died in our place, so that when we agree that we have failed him, He will forgive us and make our lives new. So I realized that Good Friday is called good because of what Christ had done and that He did it for me."

I cannot explain what took place through this experience, but I know that my heart was warmed toward my Creator God and I sensed, and still sense, that He is real and that He speaks to me by making a deep impression in my inner being. And changes took place in my life. At Thornes House we all took Scripture classes. My grades in Scripture class had been mediocre up to that time. But they became quite good. I took an elective course, "Scripture Knowledge," and passed the exam for it for the general certificate of education. I felt the call to be a lay minister, although at that time I did not really know what it meant. And I now had a deep sense of right and wrong. Whenever I did anything wrong it bothered me and I found out that I had to confess it to be at peace again.

Then my love of nature intensified. All the things I had come to enjoy; the outdoors, the sunsets, gardening, animals, and hiking took on greater beauty and interest.

And I was ready for new adventures, even bigger and better than those before. Some of these were to come during the summer breaks from school just after my fourteenth and fifteenth birthdays

13

SUMMER BREAKS

One of my older sisters, Ethel, had married and her husband Colin was in the British Navy and was stationed near Winchester in Southern England. I was approaching my fourteenth birthday when they invited me to stay with them for a month during my summer break from school. I had not been that far south so I was glad to have an opportunity to explore new territory. I had a six week summer break so I would be able to fit it in quite nicely.

So I packed and took the bus from Wakefield to Pontefract, then the passenger train from Pontefract to Winchester, a distance of about 250 miles.

The naval base was out in the country so I had a lot of leisurely days exploring the fields and streams nearby then coming home for a delicious meal prepared by my sister. There was one incident on that trip, though, that stands out in my memory and that of my sister. There was a field of wheat across the road from the base, and it was harvest time. So a special ritual took place. The harvesting machine began by going around the perimeter of the field, then continued to go round and round, working

45

towards the center. Hearing the noise of the machine, all the animals that lived in the field moved towards the center until they were crowded into a smaller and smaller space. Then they started running out. A number of us were ready with sticks. A hare came running out near me, so I chased it, Zig zag, zig zag. I knew that hares were fast runners, but I didn't know that they kept changing direction as they ran. Finally I caught it, but I just couldn't kill it. One of the men in the group killed it for me. So triumphantly I took it home. Ethel and Colin were not at home so I proudly placed the hare on the dining room table. When Ethel came home, she almost fainted, but Colin took the hare, dressed it, and we had hare stew the next day for dinner.

While staying at the Naval Base, I often walked or took the bus to Winchester, with its beautiful cathedral and gardens, and I attended church there. One day I took a train ride to London and explored the City. Another time I took a ride to Portsmouth and Southampton, both of which were on the south coast of England. My visit to Portsmouth, though, is deeply etched in my memory. It had been eight years since the end of World War II, but there were still bombed out buildings and block after block after block of buildings all laid flat.

But the month went by - a wonderful month with a loving sister and her husband and more great memories and adventures. It was time to go back north. It was time to return to Thornes House. It was time to start planning an even bigger adventure for the next and final summer break in the Thornes House experience.

14

A FIVE HUNDRED MILE HIKE

y the time I was fifteen, I was ready, not only for more adventure, but also to meet great challenges. Here was my last six week summer break coming up - a great opportunity to do something special. The summer before, I had been away from home for a month, so why not go away from home for a month again? I was used to hiking twenty-five miles a day for one or two days at a time, then coming home and sleeping for thirteen hours. But why not see if I could walk twenty-five miles a day for ten days at a time? I had seen southern England the summer before, so how about seeing new territory, going north to Scotland?

The plan unfolded. I mapped out the two hundred fifty mile distance from Wakefield, Yorkshire, to Edinburgh, Scotland, with overnight stays at Youth Hostels along the way, then a one week stay at the Youth Hostel in Edinburgh, then the two hundred fifty mile trek back home. I wrote about that trip for the Thornes House magazine, the *Stork*:

""No Lifts by Request"
The Town Hall clock struck twelve as I reached the boundary of Wakefield. Already my shoulders ached from the unaccustomed weight of my tightly packed rucksack, and my heart missed a beat as, for the first time, I realised the size of the task before me.

"Whatever had inspired me to walk to Edinburgh and back?" I wondered, as sucking glucose tablets, I hopefully plodded on. In the late afternoon a thunderstorm added to my discomfort, and I was so tired when at last I reached Burley Woodhead Youth Hostel, that I went straight to bed.

The next day I slowly made my way up Wharfedale to Linton Youth Hostel. All day long my legs and feet ached. As I recalled Wordsworth's words, "When like a roe I bounded o'er the mountains" and thought of my own plodding, I wondered where Wordsworth obtained such energy.

Day after day I wended my way northwards, visiting cafes and inns to drink gallons of tea, and surviving almost entirely on canned beans. Generally, I kept to the country lanes, as footpaths, now rarely used, were difficult to follow, even with a large scale map. Each day six or seven vehicles would stop alongside me and the drivers would ask whether I wanted a lift. Sometimes I would be asked when it was pouring with rain, but somehow, I always managed to refuse lifts.

One night I went to sleep on the grass verge at the side of the road. I awoke around 3:00 a.m. wet with the early morning dew. There was nothing to do but to start walking again until I could go to sleep with the help of the early morning sun.

After seven days' hard walking, I reached Berwick and crossed the border, spending my first night in Scotland at Coldingham Youth Hostel. One night I asked a farmer for permission to sleep in his barn, and was sitting on my bed of hay and sacks when I saw a small animal scurry across the floor on to my bed. It was a rat. Over an hour passed that night before I could get to sleep. At Haddington, eighteen miles from Edinburgh, I was delayed by an insect bite that had turned septic. Later, at Macmerry, I was asked to spend the night at the home of the Scottish junior mile champion, Hunter Watson.

The next day I reached Edinburgh, eleven days after leaving Wakefield.

I hold happy memories of the week that I spent in Edinburgh. The Festival was in full swing, and each day the gaily clad pipers would march down Princes Street, stop in front of the National Gallery and play such delightful airs as "The Skye Boat Song" and "Wi' a hundred pipers an' all." Throngs of happy people filled the streets, and children were singing and dancing in Princes Street Gardens. Hunter Watson ran in the Highland Games at Murrayfield with such well-known milers as John Landy. At the Youth Hostel, the common room rang with voices of all nationalities, and I talked with people from all over the world; French, Americans, Chinese, Germans, Norwegians and Swedes were only a few of the overseas visitors to the Festival. One night, at the hostel, a young Norwegian produced a banjo and began to croon, but the neighbours complained of the noise and he had to stop.

Alas! too soon, my week in Edinburgh was ended. It was time to begin the long and arduous journey back to Wakefield, which I reached in ten days.

Brian Thompson"

On my return, the local newspaper, *The Wakefield Express,* interviewed me and then published an article about my trip and printed my picture. But my wonderful days at Thornes House were coming to an end and there was coming a time of great transition in my life.

15

A YEAR OF TRANSITION

My life at Thornes House had been idyllic and I would have liked to have stayed until age eighteen and then gone on to college, but I realized that it was out of reach for our poor family. Besides, I was ready for a major change, something new and exciting, but what? In my final year at Thornes House I had also taken lessons by correspondence from the British Institute of Technology to get training to become a civil engineer. I had figured that being a civil engineer I would spend a lot of time outdoors, which I loved. But on top of my regular school work and all of my other activities, it was slow going.

I had a longing to explore other places. I had seen some of Southern England and some of Scotland, so where else could I go that was new and exciting? At that time a lot of people were emigrating from England to Australia, where they could get governmental assistance in getting started. But there was a stigma about Australia. Australia had started out as a penal colony and, right or wrong, I had a negative feeling about that place. Then I thought about Canada but I didn't have any positive feelings about Canada either. My mother told me that she had an uncle, Peter Salt, in East Liverpool, Ohio, and suggested that I write to him. Uncle Peter quickly responded and offered to send me the passage fare. Uncle Peter had emigrated to the United States when he was young and he was glad to offer me the same opportunities that he had enjoyed.

The process began. I applied for a British passport. I applied for a visa to come to the United States and for a "green card" so I could work in the United States. I had to have a physical. There were a lot of forms to fill out and have processed. At that time the quota system was in effect whereby the number of immigrants from each country was predetermined with the objective of maintaining the same racial/cultural mix in the population of the United States. English people were mostly emigrating to Australia and some to Canada, so there was no waiting list for English people wanting to emigrate to the United States.

So what to do while this long process was taking place? After finishing at Thornes House I got a job at a local bakery as a driver's helper. We delivered bread and goodies to stores and restaurants in a wide area, going up and down many long hills. One of the drivers had an ingenious way. Going down hills he would switch off the engine to save on gas so that he had enough gas to go on a frolic of his own and visit his girlfriend before heading back to the bakery. But then the bakery decided that they did not need drivers' helpers anymore so I had to find another job. My brother in law, Geoff, owned a window cleaning business so I went to work for him. The problem was that I would often show up at his house at 9:00 a.m. and he would still be in bed so I would have to work the rounds myself. The ladders would be still in the place they were left the day before and I would carry them from house to house, then leave them somewhere by the last house.

But I went through the process: the money came from Uncle Peter, I got the passport and the visa and bought tickets for the ocean liner, the *Ivernia* of the Cunard Line. I bought a single suitcase and filled it with a few items that were precious to me. I was ready to go. I went to

52

Liverpool, England, by myself the day before sailing, just to be safe. My mother and family came the day that I sailed.

I remember being on the liner, a 22,000 ton vessel, and my mother and family being on the dock below, and waiving goodbye.

As the seemingly huge ship pulled away from the dock, a new adventure began to unfold. I was excited. I was filled with eager anticipation. I had faith.

16

TO THE FAR SIDE OF THE SEA

Then off we were, across the Irish Sea. We stopped offshore by the coast of "Ireland." A smaller vessel came alongside, bringing more passengers. Then off we went again, into the Atlantic and heading toward the far side of the sea. Life aboard the *Ivernia* was fantastic. The cabin was small, with three of us squeezed in and one small porthole, but we didn't spend much time in the cabin. Elsewhere, everything was elegant. The *Ivernia* was new and this was her maiden voyage to New York. After dining at restaurants that served things like beans on toast, spaghetti on toast and poached egg on toast, to be looking at a menu with pot-au-feu and many delicacies on it was amazing to me.

There were a lot of planned activities and shows scheduled, but I spent a lot of my time topside, enjoying the sun, the breeze, the fresh air. It was December, but there in the middle of the Atlantic it was warm due to the Gulf Stream. I spent a lot of time on the after-deck and what surprised me was that seagulls were following the *Ivernia* all the way, no doubt getting scraps of food tossed out from the dining room. Looking out over the vast ocean I wondered what America was really like and what the future would bring.

I did not get to know very well the two men who I shared the cabin with. One was a traveling salesman, an American, who had been on a business trip to Europe. The other was an Englishman who had suffered a nervous breakdown and had been told by his doctor to get away for an extended period of time, so he was going to Canada to recuperate. But I did get to know the people at my table in the dining room because we were assigned to the same seat at every meal. These were older people who had been on a leisurely trip to Europe.

After five enjoyable, memorable days, land was sighted and we put into Halifax, Nova Scotia, where we discharged some passengers. We were allowed to go on shore so I went around town with the people from my dining room table. We stopped at an eatery and had pie and tea. I had not anticipated the need to have Canadian currency on me, so the people I was with kindly paid my bill. From the little town, the *Ivernia* looked huge.

So off again, for the final segment of the trip, down along the coast to New York City. Excitement was beginning to grow in me. By now, we were away from the influence of the Gulf Stream. A severe storm developed. The *Ivernia* rolled side to side, up and down. These were the days before stabilizers were installed on ocean liners. I bought some over the counter medication for seasickness but I did not need it. Many did.

Then the storm ended. A new day dawned. The sun was shining and we were sailing into New York Harbor. I was up on deck, taking in the sights. We passed the Statue of Liberty and I was surprised that the Statue was green. The *Ivernia* docked. I was still on deck, still taking in the sights, in awe, hardly believing that, "I am here."

A woman came up to me. She was in uniform with an "S" on her collar. She asked me, "Are you Brian Thompson?" "Yes," I replied. "I've been looking all over for you," she chidingly said. It was a "Lassie" from the Salvation Army, sent as an angel to guide me through the maze of New

York City. The U.S. Immigration Service had set up a processing area on board so we went successfully through, picked up my one suitcase, left the *Ivernia*, and walked through the streets of New York City. It was a very cold day. We passed the Rockefeller Center where people were ice skating. Then we stopped at an eatery where she treated me to pie and tea. Then we went on to the bus station. I had thirty dollars in my pocket, just enough for the bus fare to Ohio with just a few dollars change. The bus came and I said goodbye to the Salvation Army "Lassie" and to New York City. That woman had been a tremendous blessing in my life - a sixteen year old in a strange land not knowing anybody on this side of the sea, yet immediately being shown kindness and love and being given direction. Sometimes people come into our lives for just a brief moment but their impact on our lives is profound.

To me the bus ride was exciting. To travel about five hundred miles by bus, going through long tunnels through mountains, was a new experience. The bus stopped in Philadelphia. I changed buses in Pittsburgh, then finally arrived at East Liverpool, Ohio.

I had traveled from Liverpool, England, to East Liverpool, Ohio.

17

LIFE AS A NEW IMMIGRANT

t was December 10, 1955, my first day in these United States of America. And now, after a ten hour bus ride, it was my first time in Ohio, my new home. My great-uncle, Peter Salt, was waiting for me when I got off the bus in East Liverpool. His friend, Bill Trelevyn, had driven him there. After a ride around the downtown area to look at the Christmas lights and decorations, we went up the long, steep hill and arrived at Uncle Peter's house.

Uncle Peter was a wonderful, kind, eighty-three year old man who lived in a small house in a neighborhood that had gravel streets and no regular sidewalks. The house had two rooms upstairs, two rooms and a bathroom downstairs, and a basement. There was a coal furnace which could heat water to warm the two downstairs rooms but the furnace was never used because Uncle Peter just lived in the kitchen and had his bed in the kitchen. There were gratings in the ceilings of the two downstairs rooms to allow some heat to go upstairs by natural convection. In the kitchen there was a big coal stove which was used for both cooking and heating. There was a small garden in which he grew a few tomatoes to sell in the neighborhood. But Uncle was a Christian who lived his faith. Often he would stop while walking across the floor and start singing. One of his favorite songs was, "Some day the silver cord will break, and I as now, no more shall sing. But O the joy when I awake, within the palace of the King."

I arrived in East Liverpool on Saturday evening, and the very next morning I walked downtown with Uncle to the Salvation Army Citadel for morning worship. At testimony time, he went up front, faced everybody and told about the work of God in his life. That same day, the lady who did some cleaning of his house stopped by. Her name was Elsie Stansbury. She was about the same age as Uncle, but very spry. She invited me to the Free Methodist Church which was just down the hill from Uncle's house.

Soon it was Christmas time. I was used to being with lots of family members at Christmas, but now it was just Uncle Peter and I. I would walk past houses that were lighted up and just long to be inside with people. I got talking with a girl in the neighborhood and she said that I could spend some time with their family, but when she checked with her parents they said no. So I was really homesick for family.

Christmas came and went. A new year dawned and it was time to make myself useful. I helped Uncle Peter around the house, bringing coal up from the basement and doing chores and shopping, but that did not take much effort or time. The U.S. Consul in England had told me that I could earn high wages in the United States so I was eager to work. But God had a better plan. I went to the local unemployment office to inquire about getting a job. The manager there told me that I would need a work permit and suggested that I go and talk with the owner of the local business school, Marie Steir. I immediately followed his suggestion and found the owner to be a kind and sympathetic woman. She consulted with her co-owner, Howard Graham, and they offered to give me free tuition in exchange for sweeping the floors, keeping the "coke" machine filled and for doing other chores around the school. I gladly accepted. I now had an opportunity to learn business methods and procedures, accounting, typing and U.S. spelling - all marketable skills.

Uncle Peter had a sister, Sarah, who lived in a tiny house in an alley downtown, so I visited her from time to time. Her house had a potbelly stove in the middle of it. But Aunt Sarah died soon after I arrived, leaving me with only one relative in town.

Now, however, my life as an immigrant was going in a positive direction and I began to develop friendships with many kind and thoughtful people. I was starting to settle in.

18

SETTLING IN

A s the months rolled on I began to adjust and take the first steps towards becoming a part of the local culture. At first, to be understood, I had to repeat myself three times. My mixed accent and different manner of expression was difficult for people to follow. So I worked hard at trying to pick up the local way of speaking and soon I was having to repeat myself only once or not at all. I even auditioned at the East Liverpool radio station, WOHI, for a position as an announcer. I did not get the job, but I enjoyed trying and I felt that I needed part time work. There were two major employers in the area. The largest employer was Midland Steel, which was a few miles up the Ohio river at Midland, Pennsylvania. The next largest was a pottery, Hall China. Across the river from East Liverpool, in Chester, West Virginia, there was a building, a gift shop, that was in the shape of a gigantic teapot and was a tourist attraction. But I needed something that fitted into my schedule at Ohio Valley Business College, an after school job. So I first went to work at a bowling alley. This turned out to be what I consider to have been my worst job ever. This was in the days before automatic pin setters. I sat above the pins. Then, when players knocked the pins over, I would jump down and set them up again, over and over again. Besides not liking the job, the pay was terrible. I was paid by the frame, and it worked out to about thirty-five cents per hour. So I lasted just a few days, then quit.

But then I took a job with the local newspaper, the East Liverpool Review. After school I would go to the plant, and while the presses were running, I and several others would be rolling up newspapers and preparing them for mailing. My supervisor, Ralph Deshler, was very kind to me. He gave me a penknife that really was both a knife and a pen. I still have it and use it to this day. Sometimes at the newspaper I would go as a driver's helper delivering newspapers around all of the communities in the area. And I worked in the office doing typing for a special mailing they were sending out.

My fellow students at the business school were kind, too. One, Bill, gave me the clothes he had worn at his wedding: a light pinkish jacket, light pants and tie. So I stood out as I walked around town - most everyone else wore jeans. A local tailor gave me a few clothes, including a belt. I was blessed. Although I had a much lower standard of living than I had expected, the kindness and generosity of my new found friends more than made up for it.

The people at the church and at the Salvation Army were good to me as well, and I became more and more involved. Sunday became a busy day for me. In the morning I would be at the Free Methodist Church for Sunday School class and morning worship. Then, in the afternoon, I would teach eight and nine year olds in Sunday School at the Salvation Army. Then, in the evening, at the Church our young peoples' group would give a half-hour service, followed by the Sunday evening evangelistic service. Sometimes I would lead the young peoples' service. The men of the Church would touch me on the shoulder and that would encourage me. The Pastor, W.P. Jones, befriended me, so when he held evangelistic services out of town, I would travel there and back each evening. The people in the Church paid for me to spend a week at Fairchance, Pennsylvania, at the church youth camp there. I made new friends at Fairchance, including a boy preacher, Rich Stevick, and was drawn to a closer walk with God. The other boys at the camp marveled because I was the only one who wore pajamas to bed.

So I was really settling in and adjusting. I was advancing through education. I was finding fulfillment through teaching Sunday School and sometimes leading the young peoples' services. I was growing spiritually through Bible reading, sitting in Sunday School and listening to sermons. But there was still a little void - the need to have a close companion. That need was soon to be met.

19

PROS AND CONS

One thing that I missed a lot when I first came to the United States was hiking and youth hosteling. I had become used to following the many public footpaths across farmers' fields, over styles and across the moors and along the cliffs beside the North Sea, and staying at hostels for a few cents a night. But here there was none of it. I tried hiking along the country roads but traffic was heavy and I concluded that it was a dangerous undertaking. Also there was not the inexpensive and expansive bus service and rail service to get me to any parks where I could hike. I thought about hiking the entire Appalachian Trail, but that would take a lot of planning which would take a lot of time, maybe a year. Soon, however, I would meet someone and a new phase of my life would come.

More and more I was adjusting and really enjoying Ohio and the United States of America. After growing up in a climate where the summers were cool and rainy (it often would rain every day for a whole week), to come to a place where there was a lot of summer sunshine was simply wonderful. And here when it rained it would usually be a heavy rain of short duration instead of a continual light rain or drizzle. In England I had often hiked across the moors in a scotch mist, like a heavy, wet fog. I had just accepted it and lived with it as being normal.

Then I enjoyed color. I am so glad that God created color. He could have made everything just black and white and shades of gray, but He lovingly gave us color to enjoy. As I was growing up, all of the cars were black. Most of the clothes were dark because of the soot which rained down from the chimneys of houses and factories, and the schools and hospitals, etc., were painted medium green and medium brown. And here I was walking around East Liverpool, Ohio, in my newly acquired bright wedding clothes and seeing people, when they were dressed up, in bright array. Also I enjoyed the brightly colored cars. It was still in the middle fifties, when cars were often painted in two colors. My favorite was, and still is, the '55 Mercury. There were also a lot of '55 Bel Airs and '55 Ford Fairlanes. I liked the DeSotos as well. In England, to own a house and a car was the ultimate dream. Here it was an expectation, and I began to have longings to be driving, to own a home with a garden, and to have a family. My Uncle Peter's friend, William Trelevyn, offered to give me driving lessons. He owned a panel truck with stick shift. He gave me a first lesson out at Thompson Park. Then he concluded that his insurance did not cover me, became uneasy about it, and that was the end of the driving instruction with him.

Uncle Peter inspired me. He was a man of strong faith. Here he was, eighty-three years old, missing his wife who had died several years before, living alone, limited in what he could do, but enjoying life as he communed with God. One thing I liked about him was his steadfastness. He was always kind to me and encouraged me. Uncle Peter had a son, Lester, and grandchildren living in Tonawanda, New York, but Lester only came to visit his dad once while I lived in East Liverpool and did not contact him regularly. The memory that I have of my Uncle Peter, which is fixed firmly in my mind, is of the many times when I came home that I would enter the tiny back porch and look through the window of the kitchen door and there I would see Uncle Peter kneeling at his bedside, praying. Of course I would wait to enter until he had finished his prayers and that often was a long time.

Soon I would meet a special friend. With that and all of these positives there is little wonder that I started and successfully completed a citizenship course by correspondence from Ohio State University. This was the first step towards naturalization.

20

ROMANCE AT SEVENTEEN

One day, as I was walking down the long hill, a car pulled up alongside of me and the driver offered me a ride to downtown East Liverpool, so I hopped in. The driver said that he was "Bud" Swan and I discovered that he lived on the same block of Oak Street where I lived. When I told him that I was attending Ohio Valley Business College he told me that he had a daughter, Arlene, who had just graduated from High School and would now be attending Ohio Valley.

Sure enough, Arlene appeared at the Business School and I immediately introduced myself. From that point on it was Brian and Arlene. We would walk to school together five days a week and be in some classes together. The school was on the second floor of a building in the center of town. Stores were on the first floor. There was no air conditioning, so on hot days we would open all of the windows early in the morning to let the cool air in, then close them later to keep the hot air out. The third floor was vacant and was partly used for storage. But also on the third floor was an upright piano. After class, the owner of the school would let Arlene and I go up there for a while, while I practiced playing the piano. I also did chores at the school in exchange for tuition so I was at the school on Saturday mornings to sweep the floor and clean up. Arlene would join me, and after the chores were done, the owner, Marie, would get out the donuts and we would all have an enjoyable social time together.

Sunday mornings we were together as well. Arlene was with me in Sunday School and Morning Worship. There was an active Youth Group at Church and we were a part of it. We often went on trips, like to Pittsburgh airport and to Youth Rallies and had social activities at various homes. I went on a day trip to Conneaut, Ohio, with Arlene and her parents. Then in the evenings I would often be at her parents' house and Arlene and I would sit on the couch together, watching television. We both joined Avondale Free Methodist Church together as members on Easter Sunday, 1957. I don't believe that Arlene and I ever officially dated, but as you can see, we didn't need to.

Then things began to change. I remember standing on Uncle Peter's front porch one day. Arlene was standing on the sidewalk. We were talking and Arlene was smiling in the cute manner that she had. I thought, "I could never love anyone the way I love Arlene." About the same time, I was wearing out my welcome at Arlene's house. Her dad would come downstairs in his pajamas at about 11:30 in the evening and turn the television off. I was not used to sign language, so it happened a few more times, then I was forbidden to go over there. All of this happened shortly before I was set to graduate from the business school and everything was about to change for both Arlene and I, so what was going to happen?

I did not understand it fully at the time, but now I see that God was using the owner of the business school, Marie Steir, as His instrument to work everything out. Arlene was suddenly pulled out of the school and moved to Cleveland, Ohio, where she lived at the YWCA on Franklin Boulevard and took a job at a big department store, Higbee Company. I now believe that Marie told Arlene's parents that they should send Arlene to the City because of the opportunities there. Perhaps Arlene's parents thought that it would be good for her to be a long way from Brian and it would break the relationship. After all, what good could a poor immigrant boy do for their only daughter?

At the same time, matchmaker Marie told me that Arlene would make a good wife for me and that I should move to Cleveland when I graduated and take advantage of all the opportunities that life in the big city had to offer.

In my heart I knew that I was headed in the right direction. I was filled with faith and determination.

21

MARRIAGE AT EIGHTEEN

Arlene and I were physically about one hundred miles apart, but our hearts were close together. Marie let us use the Post Office box that the school had, so we wrote love letters to each other every day. Marie had entrusted me with making the daily bank deposits and picking up the mail for the school, so I had immediate access to all of Arlene's letters and I could mail my letters to her while I was at the Post Office. But writing letters each day was not enough. On Fridays, right after working for the East Liverpool Review, I would hop onto a Greyhound bus, spend a few short hours with Arlene, then take a Trailways bus back to East Liverpool, arriving in the wee hours of the morning. Then a few hours of sleep and off to sweep the floor at the school. It was all like a wonderful dream.

Soon it was time to graduate from Ohio Valley Business College. The big day arrived. Marie had asked me to play some marching music on the piano at the ceremony. I had practiced diligently and I was ready. About the only thing I remember about that ceremony was that I played the whole piece well as the graduates walked forward but when I got to the end of the piece, the students were still walking and I froze. I didn't know what to do. Nobody told me that I should go back to the beginning and continue playing. Marie came running over and frantically tried to get me to play more, but I just couldn't. I felt badly that I had let Marie down, but my mind quickly moved on to the adventures and challenges that lay just ahead.

Working at my part-time job, earning a little more than a dollar an hour, I had saved about two hundred dollars so I was ready to move. Across the street from the YWCA where Arlene was staying, there was a YMCA where I could stay for two dollars fifty cents a night. It was just perfect. So I packed all of my belongings into my one suitcase again, said a few goodbyes and took the Greyhound bus to Cleveland and moved into the YMCA. My room at the YMCA was tiny - just enough room for a single bed, a small desk and a dresser. There was a central shower room and dining room - but it was adequate for my needs at the time. Not too far away was a Royal Castle where I could get a small hamburger for sixteen cents, french fries and Birch beer (Root beer).

The first objective was for me to find employment so I signed up with an employment agency and they arranged for me to go on job interviews in the downtown area. The YMCA was about a mile and a half from downtown - an easy walk for me. I bought a weekly bus pass, so in between interviews I rode all around the city and suburbs getting to know the entire area. Marie had told me to ask for three hundred dollars a month and one offer I had from the electric company was for two hundred seventy-five dollars a month, which I turned down. After going on several interviews it seemed that two hundred seventy-five dollars was all that I was going to get, so when I was offered about that amount by Carrier Corporation, I accepted. I would be working in the branch office on Superior Avenue in Cleveland as an accounts payable clerk and bookkeeping machine operator. My job hunting experience had taken about ten days and I was ready to take the next step.

Now I needed to arrange more permanent housing. I don't know how I ended up at East 65th Street and Euclid, but I saw an apartment building there with a "for rent" sign out front. So I went inside and made inquiries. Imagine my surprise when the lady manager said to me, "Oh, we'se black," and wouldn't rent to me because I was white! But just around the corner on East 65th Street was a large house that had been converted into a rooming house and I was able to rent space there for a reasonable amount.

I don't believe that I ever proposed to Arlene, but we both new that marriage was right for us. I had just turned eighteen years old and Arlene had turned eighteen the prior October. To get married in Ohio without parental consent we would have to be twenty-one years old. So I did some research at the library and found out that we could be married in Michigan at age eighteen, but there would be a three-day wait after filing the application before the marriage could be officiated. I stopped at a law office on West 25th Street and the lawyer there told me that there would be no obstacle to us going to Michigan and getting married there.

So we hopped on a Greyhound bus and went to Detroit. Arlene stayed at the YWCA there and I stayed close by at the YMCA. We filed the application right away and had the required blood tests taken, then did some sightseeing until the three days were up, and then picked up our license. We were married on July 6, 1957, by Judge Dingelman.

Starry-eyed and with great expectations we hopped on a Greyhound bus again and headed back to Cleveland.

22

A PLACE OF NEW BEGINNINGS

B ack in Cleveland, back at the YWCA and YMCA, we didn't waste any time. I packed my one suitcase once again and Arlene got her belongings ready. Then we called for a taxi. I placed my one suitcase in the taxi. Arlene brought one batch of belongings out, then another, then another. The cab driver became annoyed at us for using the taxi as a moving truck. He complained all the way to our new home and didn't seem happy at the amount of the extra tip I gave him. Our new home was an average sized furnished room with a double bed in the middle. There was a tiny kitchenette and a tiny bathroom with a shower. But we were deeply in love and any place together was wonderful. Besides, there was a front porch that ran across the entire front of the house. It had chairs, including a big rocking chair that I loved. So we could escape the confines of the small room from time to time.

We had made connections with the First Free Methodist Church and had attended there for a week or two, so newly-found friends from the church, Dick and Bertha Crookham, gave us a ride to church the very next morning, then gave us lunch at their apartment. They lived about a mile from us in a neighborhood named Hough. The church was small. The sanctuary seated about one hundred and twenty people (if they sat close together in the pews) with a semi-circular altar rail, piano and organ in front. In the basement was a seated area with small classrooms all around. The pastor's name was Milford Casto who had worked for a bank before becoming a pastor. The pastor, his wife, and everyone in the church were very friendly so we quickly made good friends. Many of the people in the church had recently moved to Cleveland from Pennsylvania, West Virginia and Southern Ohio to work in the automobile and steel making facilities and to take advantage of the opportunities that the big city had to offer. Several came from the Uniontown area of Pennsylvania, not too far from East Liverpool. So I quickly felt at home and was soon teaching eight year olds in Sunday School. Within a week or two of our marriage, the church gave us a wedding shower with many gifts for us that we greatly appreciated. George and Eileen Crookham became very good friends of ours and they took us down to the Church Conference Campground on Route 39 just outside of Mansfield, Ohio, where we spent a weekend staying with them in their small cabin. The Crookham's were two brothers, Dick and George, who had married two sisters, Bertha and Ilene, so we were all special friends.

I started my job at Carrier Corporation and it proved to be a great blessing. Carrier was in process of air conditioning many of the large buildings downtown so it turned out to be a very secure position. I had a small office where I processed bills from suppliers. I had to get various approvals, code the bills with account numbers, then prepare them in batches for accounting entry and submission to headquarters in Syracuse, New York, for payment. The accounting entry I did on a gigantic Burroughs bookkeeping machine. I inserted record cards into the machine, punched keys and the carriage moved back and forth posting the entries. It was a little complicated, but I quickly mastered all of this and it became routine. This was my first full-time job and I was not used

80

to working closely with a large group of people. I was from a different culture so it was a big adjustment for me and I ruffled a few feathers.

But I learned to pray individually for each person I worked with and everything smoothed out. I was put in charge of the candy machine. Just as I had filled the "Coke" machine at the business school, so now I kept the candy machine filled at Carrier. It seems, though, that the biggest problem I had at Carrier was that my office did not have any windows and I was under fluorescent lights looking at a moving machine carriage. The branch office was a long narrow building with only two windows right at the front of the building. At lunchtime, I would stand at one of those front windows, looking out and longing to be out there.

So I was adjusting to life in the big city and we were adjusting to married life and we were making friends.

Great times and new experiences were ahead.

23

SETTLED IN

One good thing about Carrier Corporation was that a tuition refund program was available to employees. Also, Fenn College, which later became Cleveland State University, was just a few blocks away. So a few weeks after starting at Carrier I stopped in at Fenn College and met with the Dean of Business Administration. I did not have a regular high school diploma but the Dean was very kind and told me that I could start classes on probation and see how well I did. He said that I would not be given any credit for Business School, but that the business school lessons would be very helpful to me. So in the fall of 1957 I started classes at Fenn College, two evenings each week, four hours each evening. I decided to take all of my accounting classes near the beginning because they would help me advance in my daytime job. That first term I took Accounting 101 and an English grammar class and did well. The only hard part at Fenn College was that my early classes were held on the second floor of the Tower and the hallways had very low ceilings. Back in those days almost everyone smoked, so during the ten minute breaks the hallways were heavy with smoke, which was hard on a non-smoker like me.

My boss at Carrier, Les Binder, surprised me. One day I was sick with the flu so I called in sick. Arlene was with me. Suddenly, who comes to the door but Les Binder. Arlene let him in and he saw that I was sick and in bed. After that, he trusted me completely. Les said that he had caught a lot of employees in the past lying about being sick. Les and I became friends.

Now that we were both working and had some spending money we were able to get foods that I had not been able to afford before. I had a sweet tooth and I liked ice-cream and especially liked ice-cream floats. I over indulged on ice-cream floats and became tired of them. We were not wealthy but we were not big spenders. We were able to live on my income and deposit Arlene's income into a savings account. For budgeting, we used the envelope system. We had an envelope for rent, an envelope for food, etc. So when I cashed my paycheck I would split up the currency and place it in the appropriate envelopes. One envelope I had was for what we called "advancement." The money in that envelope was used for my tuition, and later for furniture. Carrier reimbursed me for only seventy five percent of my tuition, and only after I showed good grades.

We had settled into a regular routine. I worked at Carrier five days a week, Monday through Friday, nine to five, with evening classes two nights a week at Fenn College. Arlene worked late morning until evening at Higbees. On the evenings when I did not have class I would take the bus to Higbees and meet her after work, then we would go home together. On Saturdays we would get groceries, do cleaning and go on little trips around town, like the zoo or Euclid Beach Park which was an amusement park with a beach on the shore of Lake Erie. The east side of Cleveland had some trolley busses which had wheels but were powered by an overhead electric cable. Once in a while the bus would lose contact with the cable. Then the driver would have to get out and reconnect it. On Sundays we were in Sunday School and Morning Worship, then after a power nap we were back in the evening for Evening Worship. Arlene helped with the small children in Sunday School.

One weekend, soon after our marriage, we took a bus ride to East

Liverpool to patch up our relationship with Arlene's family. We stayed with her aunt and uncle who lived not far from Oak Street, where her parents and Uncle Peter lived. We stopped and visited Uncle Peter for a while. He seemed to be getting along fine. Then we stopped at her parents' house. We didn't say very much but we waived the olive branch. It was like, "Here we are. We are married. We both have jobs and we are doing fine." I don't think that they knew what to say. We left on a good note. We visited other family and friends, for the first time as husband and wife.

In the back of my mind, I had thought that I would come to America and try it for two years. Amazingly, and with the guidance and providence of God, I had completed business school, married, settled in a good job, enrolled in college, settled in a good church, signed up for the draft and successfully completed citizenship classes by correspondence, all within the first two years. I was really settled in.

24

MOVING FORWARD

We soon realized that we had moved into a "not so desirable" part of town. We were in a higher crime area. Our sleep was often interrupted by the sound of sirens and it did not seem safe to go out walking in the neighborhood, especially in the evenings. Besides that, the place that we were staying had roaches and mice. It was not a place where we could entertain company. The only advantage was that it was a short bus ride to work for Arlene and a short ride home from Fenn College for me. But the bad outweighed the good, so after six months, having saved some money, we decided to move.

We found an unfurnished basement apartment available for forty five dollars per month. It was on West 57th Street between Detroit Avenue and Franklin Boulevard and just a five minute walk from church and a short bus ride to downtown. It was ideal for us at that time, so we took it. We bought some very inexpensive furniture, but it was new. Arlene's parents came to visit us and we had enjoyable times. They liked to go downtown and enter the big department stores like May Company and Higbees where Arlene worked. On one of the top floors at Higbees there was a restaurant named the Silver Grille. In the middle of the restaurant was a large fish pond filled with large goldfish. For quite a while we ate there every time that Arlene's parents came into town.

Winter had come and gone. It had been cold standing at the bus stops, especially when the outside temperature was below zero degrees Fahrenheit, and I hadn't yet learned how to dress properly for the cold. But I knew that Spring was coming and looked forward to it. Spring came and the Spring semester at Fenn College ended. I had successfully completed the first year of my classes. I decided not to take any Summer classes because we both needed a break. It had been hard work, but we both had a feeling of accomplishment and looked forward to moving ahead some more.

Then in June of 1958, I experienced some pain in my abdomen and had some other symptoms. Something just wasn't right. One of the women in the church, Agnes Lawrence, worked for a medical doctor, Charles A. Obert. So I went to see him. He told me that I had all of the symptoms of Appendicitis and that I needed to have surgery immediately. Dr. Obert was amazing. He was not only a general practitioner but he was a surgeon, doing many kinds of surgery and delivering babies. He did not give appointments, but saw patients on an "as needed" basis. Patients would sit waiting for him, sometimes for hours, while he delivered a baby or took care of some emergency, but he would take care of every last patient, even if it got to eleven or eleven thirty at night. And he only charged three dollars per visit at that time. So I was admitted to St. John's Hospital on Detroit Avenue and Dr. Obert removed my appendix. Back in those days, it meant a hospital stay of about ten days, so I had plenty of time to rest and recover from a year of rigorous activity.

Dr. Obert had told me not to go back to work for a while, but after I was home for a couple of days, Les Binder called me and wanted me to come to work for a few hours each day. Carrier had hired a temporary worker to operate the bookkeeping machine, but she needed some training. How could I refuse? I needed to keep my job. Besides, my one-year anniversary was coming up and I would qualify for two weeks paid vacation. So he offered to drive me back and forth and I accepted. It was a little hard but I did not suffer any for it except for some discomfort. Lesley Binder really appreciated my cooperation and friendship.

While I was in the hospital, Uncle Peter died. I was not able to attend his funeral, but I look forward to being with him again after I, like him, depart this life and we are together before the Throne of God. And thank you, Uncle Peter, for sending me the passage fare so that I could come to these wonderful United States of America.

25

MORE PROGRESS

Carrier graciously paid me for my time in the hospital and recovery. I completed my first year of service and qualified for two weeks of paid vacation. We had saved some money so we wanted to get away and see more of this wonderful country. We were used to traveling on Greyhound busses and we noticed that Greyhound had a ten day travel package for a trip to Miami Beach, Florida - bus fare, hotel, sunshine, sight seeing, swimming in the ocean, etc., so we jumped at the opportunity.

It was July, 1958, and the interstate highway system had not yet been built, so it took forty hours to ride from Cleveland, Ohio, to Miami, Florida. We stayed on the same bus all the way, just stopping for meals and to drop off and pick up passengers. We had figured on sleeping on the bus during the night, but that did not work so well. During the night we were going round and round the mountains in Tennessee being swayed from side to side. But it was a big adventure and the scenery was terrific as we traveled.

Finally, we arrived in Miami, travel weary and ready for real sleep. We took a taxi ride to our hotel on Collins Avenue, and we were amazed. At that time Miami Beach was at the height of its glory. It was an extremely popular tourist destination. Collins Avenue was lined with a great many hotels, with the front facing the road and palm trees and with the back right on the beach and ocean. The weather was perfect, just an occasional convectional shower later in the day. In the morning, tour busses would come along Collins Avenue, picking up passengers from the hotels to visit various tourist attractions, including alligator wrestling. So each morning we would go on one of those tours. In the afternoons, we would put on our swim clothes and swim in the ocean and lay on the beach. We loved to jump into those ocean waves. On Sunday morning we visited the Free Methodist Church in Miami. To save money, we ate a good breakfast, had a big meal at lunch time, and just had snacks in the evening.

Alas, it was time to take another long bus ride home and return to work. My supervisor, Lesley Binder, kindly took me to lunch so I could tell him all about our trip.

That summer, we developed several new friendships. At that time, the Free Methodist Church rotated pastors frequently. Usually, a pastor stayed only one or two years at each local church. A new pastor, Fred Kreh was assigned to Cleveland First. He and his wife quickly became friends of ours. Arlene was especially friends with pastor's wife. We also befriended a girl on the next street, Eileen Schaeffer, who was in her early teens. Eileen was at our place almost every day and went on little trips with us such as to the Cleveland Zoo. She became like family. Then a couple who had emigrated from Germany moved into the top floor of our building and became friends. We often played Scrabble with them. They learned English and we learned some German from the game. Also, at that time, the evening newspaper, The Cleveland Press, offered language records for one dollar each, so I bought a German language record, played it over and over and learned some German that way.

But the strongest friendship we developed was with a young couple who lived in a rented house directly across the street from us, Jim and Charlene Mallow, who had moved up to Cleveland from Job, West Virginia, to find work. They had two small children and would go for a drive in the evening to get the children to fall asleep, so we would ride with them. Sometimes we would go to a lookout spot close to the Cleveland Airport for a while and watch the planes coming in and taking off. Jim and Charlene had just bought a used 1954 Buick automobile from a used car lot on the East Side, and we had saved up some money and I had taken driving lessons from a local driving school, Safeway. I had taken the driving test and had a license, so I was ready to go. Jim drove us to the same car lot and we found a 1954 Buick Super for nine hundred and fifty dollars. It was baby blue - Arlene's favorite color and a color that I liked also. It had a cracked driver's side window, but the salesman said to bring it back and they would fix it. So we bought it and I drove it right home. I went back a day or two later but the car lot had disappeared, but Jim kindly put in a new window for me. At age nineteen, I was a new driver.

After the easier days of summer, it was time to start my second year of night classes. I suddenly was extra busy. It was like jumping onto a moving train.

26

ON THE MOVE AGAIN

enjoyed having the '54 Buick Super, immensely. That car had a lot of chrome grille work in front and I spent hours polishing it up. The blue paint had faded quite a bit, so I had it painted at Earl Scheibe's for $29.95. It had white walled tires so it looked really good. And life was so much easier having a car - no standing out in the cold waiting for busses. We were able to visit friends easily, go sightseeing to places like Hale Historical Farm and Stan Hywet Mansion with its beautiful gardens, and attend church camp on Route 39 near Mansfield and visit family and friends in East Liverpool. I did have trouble getting car insurance at first though. My supervisor at Carrier, Lesley Binder, put me in touch with an insurance broker. I would sign up for insurance, then later get a call at work saying that the insurance company had declined to accept me. This happened two or three times. I think that the problem was that because of my age I was considered high risk, but at the same time my premium was much lower because I was married. However, Ed Cook, an agent with Nationwide Insurance, called me one evening and offered me coverage with an even lower premium, and I've had my insurance with Nationwide ever since.

That fall of 1958, and the winter and spring that followed, passed by quickly as I was busy with work and night classes and church. At church, I continued to teach eight year olds in Sunday School while Arlene continued to help with the little ones. We attended Sunday Morning Worship and the Evening Evangelistic Service. The church had a Wednesday evening prayer meeting, but I did not attend because I felt called to continue with night college courses, and between class time and homework my week night schedule was filled. My work at Carrier became repetitive and routine and was easier and easier for me. This fitted in well with night college classes and the challenges I had there. Night classes were just that. No social activities because almost all of the students worked during the day and many had family responsibilities. Despite having a busy life, I was able to get good grades and advance, building up credits, concentrating on learning accounting while taking a few other courses. In English literature class, though, I had a problem with my professor. We had to write about one piece of literature that included the Salvation Army. So I wrote about the Salvation Army as combining soap, soup, and salvation, etc. The professor wrote in red on my paper that I should not drag God into my arguments. I complained in writing to the dean, but he backed up the professor. Apparently, expressions of faith did not fit in well with what was to become a state university.

Life for us was quite busy, but it was filled with meaning and purpose which gave Arlene and I a lot of personal satisfaction. But yet, something seemed to be missing. I was one of ten children and had many nephews and nieces and loved children. In the summer of 1959 we had been married for two years and I had a strong desire to have children of my own. Arlene wanted to have children too. We felt that our basement apartment was not adequate in which to raise a family, and that we needed to be in a neighborhood that had good schools. The neighboring suburb, Lakewood, a community of some sixty thousand people, seemed ideal. Lakewood had many huge colonials that had been built in the early 1900's, and during the housing shortage of World War II many of the full attics of these colonials had been converted into apartments. So we found one of these third floor apartments that we liked and which was available. Being on the third floor, the rent was quite reasonable so we took it. The owner lived on the first floor and her sister and brother-in-law lived on the second floor.

The apartment was on Cranford Avenue, just a very short distance from the Clifton Express bus-line. The plan was that Arlene would quit her job, and I would take the bus downtown to work and night classes so that she could use the car during the daytime. Lakewood was a beautiful community with manicured lawns and many flowers. We could walk to anywhere we wanted to go - the library, the shops, and Lakewood Park which overlooked Lake Erie.

It was an answer to prayer.

27

REFLECTIONS ON OUR MARRIAGE

Our marriage at age eighteen, with no premarital counseling had been a big step of faith, but it was right for us and it was working well. Looking back, I am amazed at how different Arlene and I were. Take, for instance, our backgrounds. I had grown up in a large family, being one of ten children without a dad, and we all loved one another. Arlene had had a brother who died in infancy so she was raised as an only child with both parents, but her parents did not get along well with each other. Being in a large family, I had regularly done household chores, done shopping for the family and learned to cook and bake. On the other hand, Arlene was never allowed in the kitchen and did not do household chores or shopping. I had enjoyed a lot of freedom and independence and had traveled quite a lot, none of which Arlene had experienced.

I had worked at several jobs whereas she had never worked. I had been raised in the English culture, with such values as rugged individualism and the indomitable spirit. Arlene's parents and grandparents had all been raised here in the United States of America. And, of course, we had grown up in totally different educational systems. Arlene held a high school diploma and had attended business school for a while.

Besides having totally different backgrounds, we had completely opposite personalities. At that time in my life I was still suffering from the impact of growing up without a dad and in the midst and aftermath of an oppressive war. I had a deep seated anxiety and fears that plagued me continually. When I rode on a bus I would always try to sit by the emergency door, just in case. When I rode as a passenger in a car I would have my right hand on the door handle, ready to jump out in case of emergency. I could not sit with my back to a window, etc. Arlene was a "happy go lucky" young woman with a type A personality, outgoing, making friends easily, talkative and wanting to be around people. I was quite the opposite. Left to myself I would have been happy to stay home a lot, reading a lot, carrying "British reserve" to the extreme. I was self conscious because of my accent and was not talkative. But Arlene was to be very good for me as we made friends with other couples and I gradually came out of my shell. My work in accounting fitted my personality well. I worked with papers and numbers and did not have to interact much with people. Arlene's work in the credit office at Higbees fitted her personality well as she had plenty of interaction with people. As we faced decisions in life, I liked to plan ahead and pray and think things through, whereas she was more compulsive. But in all of the major decisions she allowed me to decide and to bear the responsibility, thus letting me be the leader in our soon to be growing family.

Even back then, I had strong faith and strong determination. I had come to faith in Christ some five years before we were married and I felt God's leading in my life. Arlene was a new believer and did not have the Biblical background that I had had growing up. When we went to bed at night, before we went to sleep, we would have a devotional time in which I would read out loud a chapter from the New Testament. I had morning and evening prayer times. I liked to spend time meditating and processing thoughts in my mind, but Arlene was not like that.

But despite all of these differences, we had a good marriage because we complemented one another. We each had our separate strengths so that, working at it together, we were strong. We loved one another deeply and we were both optimistic as we faced the future. We looked forward to having children and raising them. And we were gradually changing as we blended our lives together.

28

AN EXPANDING FAMILY

I t was not long after we settled in at 1190 ½ Cranford Avenue that Dr. Obert gave us the good news that we were expecting our first child. We were thrilled. Those were the days before ultrasound, so couples did not know the gender of their babies until the time of birth. Would it be a boy or a girl, we wondered? We would be happy either way. Dr. Obert gave us an estimated birth date in early October, which got us wondering, because Arlene's birthday was on October 6.

So all of that summer and into the fall the air was filled with expectancy and preparation. As Arlene got bigger we stayed around home a lot because she was getting uncomfortable. We went to Higbees and bought a beautiful crib and dresser set. The church gave us a baby shower. We were both ready, just waiting, waiting. Then on October 5th, as Arlene was ironing some clothes later in the day, she nonchalantly told me that her water had broken and that the time was near. In my mind, I had envisioned the baby being born in the car on the way to the hospital, so I was frantic. I hurried her up and rushed her to Fairview Hospital then waited, waited, waited.

Our baby was not born until the next day, October 6th. It was a boy, and what a birthday present for Arlene. Dr. Obert showed me my wrinkled redskin and showed me that he had all of his little fingers and toes. We were so happy! We named our son Michael, after my younger brother who had died in infancy, and we gave Michael a middle name, Allen, after Arlene's brother who had died in infancy. Back in those days, mothers and babies were kept in the hospital for several days after birthing, so I had a few quiet days, alone, making doubly sure that we were well prepared - baby bath, diapers, diaper pins, talcum powder, etc.

Then the aftershock as I brought mother and baby home. I was actually scared as I looked at this little one, so fragile and so dependent, and I was responsible for him. But I was immediately caught up with his care needs and my experience with my nephews and nieces kicked in and the scariness subsided and I was just filled with wonder and amazement at this, my son, a precious gift from God. Arlene was recovering from giving birth and had some postpartum depression, so I was helping all that I could - running diapers through our Speed Queen washer and wringer and drying on the clothes line, helping with cooking, etc. From that point on, our lives were forever changed.

Those first few months of Michael's life were extremely challenging for both of us, but with hard work and strong faith we made it through. Michael would wake up about every hour and cry all night long and we would both be up taking care of him, so we didn't get much sleep. With my full time job and night classes and homework and teaching Sunday School, my anxiety level rose and I was tense all the time. I would watch T.V. in the evening for an hour, then not know what I had watched.

But after a few months, Michael started sleeping better and everything settled down. He was a happy child and a joy to have around. We got him a little seat with wheels and he loved to race around in it. He was not yet able to walk, but he was mobile. I would be sitting on the couch, reading the newspaper, and he would race by, snatch the paper out of my hands then race away, laughing. We loved our son. Soon he was walking and getting into everything.

Arlene had a good friend, Evelyn. Evelyn and her husband, Bill, had had a son about the same time as we had Michael. So we spent many enjoyable times with them, sharing experiences. Arlene's parents enjoyed Michael and would visit from time to time. We enjoyed being parents. Our lives were even more meaningful and purposeful.

29

FIVE STEPS FORWARD

While Arlene was pregnant with Michael, who we also called Mike, I took a final step in being settled on this side of the sea. I became a United States citizen. Normally, there was a five year waiting period after arriving in this country, but for those who were married to a United States citizen, the waiting period was three years after the date of the marriage. So for me, this meant a waiting period of a few months less than five years. At the naturalization ceremony, many of the people becoming citizens were from Greece where there had been an economic upheaval soon before. The first thing I did as a citizen was to fly a United States flag from the antenna of my car. When people would ask me why I was flying it, I had quite a story to tell. I was surprised how I was immediately changed on the inside. I had been watching a lot of war movies on the television. Now, suddenly, when I saw the United States military in action I felt, "that is us."

As Mike approached his first birthday, and I had some vacation time available, we thought about how great it would be for Arlene to meet my wonderful mother and family and for them to meet Mike and Arlene.

At that time, air travel was much easier and simpler, although the travel time was somewhat longer if the airplane had turbo-prop engines instead of jet. So we took a direct flight from Cleveland to London with stops in Toronto and Scotland. So family met us at the airport and we had a wonderful time visiting and sight seeing. Mike spent his first birthday at Grandma Thompson's in England. But I was glad to get back to my new home in America.

The years were busy and seemed to be rolling along quite rapidly. It was now July of 1962 and I had worked for Carrier for five years and received my five year pin. I had attended night college classes for five years and had done well and completed most of the accounting classes. But at Carrier I was doing the same work as when I started and, being a branch office, there was no opportunity for advancement. So the Lord impressed on me that it was time to move on. I had an interview at the corporate headquarters of North American Refractories, downtown Cleveland, where there was an opening for an accounts payable clerk. The work would be similar to the work I was doing at Carrier. The pay would be about the same except that North American did not have a tuition refund program. But I sensed that there would be a lot of opportunities for advancement as I continued my education, so I accepted the position.

North American Refractories made the refractory brick and cements used in lining the steel mill furnaces, and had plants in several states. The man I interviewed with was Norman Schucard, who had started out as office boy and had climbed the corporate ladder and was now the comptroller of the company. At Carrier, I had worked in an office by myself and with no windows. Here, I was in a big room with ten people and on the tenth floor with a view of the city. North American occupied the entire tenth floor of the National City - East Sixth building. When I started at North American, we had a seven and a half hour work day with a fifteen minute break in the morning and a fifteen minute break in the afternoon - thirty five hours per week. It was easy. I adjusted to the new work environment and began making friends.

About this time, Arlene developed health problems. Her dad was diabetic and Arlene's blood sugar count became borderline high. Her dad had heart problems and Arlene's blood pressure became borderline high. But the bigger problem was her thyroid issues. One effect of this was that she did not have regular menstrual periods. One day in the summer of 1963, she was laying on the bed with her abdomen uncovered. I looked and thought I saw something moving. I looked again and it was confirmed. I told her, "We're pregnant."

Looking back, it amazes me how everything has worked out in my life - the timing, the opportunities, the advancement. I can only credit it to Divine intervention and the answers to prayers. Sometime before finding out about this second pregnancy, an elderly couple who owned a house two houses away from us had asked us if we wanted to buy their house because they wanted to move to Florida and said that they were willing to wait until we were financially able to buy it. Our third floor apartment was not suitable for raising two children and here was an opportunity to have a house of our own. Arlene's parents graciously helped us with the down payment and we happily moved to 1200 Cranford Avenue.

30

MORE STEPS FORWARD

Having a house of our own was like a dream come true. In the newspapers as I was growing up was an advertisement that declared the ultimate goal was to have a house, a car and a future. It was just part of my goal, but we had attained it. Now I had a yard to tend to and could follow my love of gardening by planting flowers and vegetables. There was a big climbing rose bush in the back that gave a profuse, bountiful display of bright red blossoms each year. There was a porch that ran across the entire front of the house and had a metal glider on it. Across the front of the porch, in place of a railing, there were flower boxes in which I planted petunias which trailed over the boxes and were a magnificent sight. If I felt hemmed in in the house, I could sit on the glider reading, doing homework and talking to people as they passed by on the sidewalk which was just a few steps away.

The previous owners, the Shimolas, had left behind all of their furniture for us, including a black upright piano which I often played and always treasured. Then there was a gardening book which I still use today, and a Zell's encyclopedia, printed in 1860, which I often still use, especially to find out deep meanings of words. The house seemed huge to me, having four bedrooms, full attic, full basement and a three car garage.

Dr. Obert did not know the date of conception, but estimated that our second baby would be born sometime in October. So we wondered - could it happen again? Would it be a girl or another boy? We had enjoyed Mike so much that we would have enjoyed having another boy. But having a girl would be enjoyable too, then we would have one of each. Memories come to me of Arlene spoon feeding baby food to Mike. When she would get the spoon to Mike's mouth, Arlene's mouth would open wide. It always seemed funny to me.

The big day came. It was time to go to Fairview Hospital. It was late evening. I felt no need to rush. We drove to the hospital, then sat in the car in the parking lot until a few minutes after midnight so the hospital would not charge for the previous day. The waiting time was not as long as it had been with Mike. Another wrinkled little one came into the world. We had a baby girl. We named her Elizabeth, after Queen Elizabeth of England and gave her the middle name Ann, another name of royalty. Elizabeth, who we called Beth, was a lot easier on us. She slept well at nights and we had had hands on experience with Mike. And Arlene was able to carry on most of the personal care of Beth.

Meanwhile, at North American, I was making good progress. The comptroller, who had interviewed me, recognized that he needed help with various accounting projects and that I had the accounting training and aptitude and could help him. So he took me from my accounts payable desk in the corner of the room and sat me at a desk at the front of the room, facing everybody, but where he could get to me easily. My new position carried a lot more responsibility but my pay was increased substantially. My only problem was that I had no job description, but I was to help not only the comptroller, Norman Schucard, but also the treasurer, Mr. Valente and the assistant comptroller, Bill Alexander. I had three bosses at the same time! If Bill or Mr. Valente wanted me to do something I often had to say, "Mr. Schucard has me doing this," then they would say, "Oh." It was quite a feat to keep all three bosses happy and it took me quite a while to get over my self-consciousness sitting facing everybody.

In night college classes I had completed the equivalent of two full time years of college and earned the associate degree. I now felt led to seek becoming a Certified Public Accountant, which at that time could be attained before earning a four year degree provided that all of the accounting courses had been successfully completed.

At church, I had taught eight year olds for several years and never thought I would be able to teach an adult class. I thought that I had too much anxiety and could not speak well or relate well. But all of these doubts did not come from my Creator and I knew that as a teenager I had been called to be a lay minister. So when I was asked to teach the senior adult class, I accepted.

I prayed a lot for strength and ability and prepared well. For a long time I would have dry heaves from anxiety on Sunday mornings before teaching, but I finally adjusted and grew spiritually and gained much personal satisfaction from being of service to my Lord. That experience of responding to difficult questions helped me greatly later in life, as you, the reader, will see later in this book.

31

TRAVEL ADVENTURES

With more responsibilities at work, a deeper ministry at church, continued night classes, two children and a wife to care for and interact with and a house and yard to maintain and improve, it was an extremely busy time from September through May, but we took advantage of the easier days of Summer. We went on many picnics and went swimming at places like Hinckley Lake, Wallace Lake and Findlay State Park. We especially liked to go to the Blue Hole in Castalia, Ohio, and picnic there and feed the fish.

One of my aunts died and left me some money, so we were able to buy a cottage on the Church Campground and we were able to attend Family Camp where we had social times as well as religious services, Bible studies and prayer times, and made many friends. Mike and Beth attended childrens' camps there and I often drove groups of children there from church. One time, when I drove a group of children there, one of the boys I took got fearful and homesick the moment we arrived, so I had to bring him right back home! When our children were at camp it was a blessing for Arlene and I as we were able to have some quiet times together. One time, when I took Beth to Family Camp, right away she broke out with large sores on her face and back. I took her to the camp nurse, Lorene Ensminger, who diagnosed the malady as being chickenpox. So right back home again we went. Family Camp was a wonderful experience for me, especially later on when my work schedule did not interfere, and I was able to spend entire weeks there and not just weekends. Being away from most responsibilities I was able to meditate and receive Divine instruction for the year ahead.

Also, as Mike and Beth grew older, we were able to travel some. We enjoyed the spectacular Niagara Falls and all of the attractions there. In 1967, there was an International Exposition in Montreal, Canada. We first stopped to visit Arlene's aunt and uncle in New York State then up to Montreal. The exposition attracted thousands of people from around the world and many residents opened up their homes to provide bed and breakfast privileges to visitors. We stayed with a French speaking family and took the subway to Expo '67 each day. I had had five years of French at Thornes House, so I started speaking French to people in this city of French speaking Quebec, but surprisingly, I was met mostly with just stares. I found out that people in Quebec speak an old style of French that is quite different from European French. The five hundred mile drive back to Lakewood from Montreal was quite arduous. I got tired of driving on the interstate system so I took the regular roads through New York State, which made it a longer trip time-wise. Mike and Beth often would get thirsty, so we would stop to get something to drink. Then they would drink too much, and we would have to stop frequently for that. Finally, we arrived home about six o'clock in the morning, exhausted, but glad to be home.

The most momentous trip, especially for Mike and Beth, but probably also for Arlene, was our trip to England as a family. Mike was about nine years old and Beth about six. At that time the greater family had grown, and Mike and Beth had about twenty one cousins, eight uncles, seven aunts, as well as the extended family, spending time with a loving caring family and Grandmother Thompson at the center of it all. Living in Lakewood, Mike and Beth had developed many friendships, at church, at camp, in the neighborhood and at school, but only had me and Arlene, Grandpa and Grandma Swan and a few distant others as family. So it was really great for them to visit and play and interact with and eat fish and chips with all of their relatives in Yorkshire. At that time all of the family still met together at Grandmother Thompson's house. We had not much time for sightseeing but plenty of time to spend together. Arlene and I, Mike and Beth did take a memorable trip to London. One of my favorite photographs is that of Arlene, Mike and Beth on Westminster Bridge with Big Ben in the background. The days passed by quickly and we returned home. As much as I enjoyed visiting England, I was always happy to return to the United States where I had been blessed with much freedom and many opportunities.

32

MOVING ALONG AT NORTH AMERICAN

had left Carrier and made a lateral move to North American, seeking greater opportunities. At the time, I did not realize how great an opportunity my Creator God was leading me into. The Comptroller, Norman Schucard had carved out a special position for me. Every assignment he gave me presented a new challenge, but I performed well. He and I enjoyed a special relationship. He had raised his sons already. I had grown up without a father. Even though we were only together during work hours, he was to me like a substitute dad. I think he treated me somewhat as another son, watching out for me and giving me some encouragement and raising my pay from time to time. He put up with my personality issues and I learned not to see him in his office too early in the morning, before he had his coffee and read the *Wall Street Journal*.

Mr. Schucard, as he was known, knew that I was intending to sit for the CPA Exam and seek to be licensed as a Certified Public Accountant so he kept checking my progress. The night college was offering a CPA exam preparation course, three hours every Friday evening for the entire academic year, so I signed up for it. It was extremely helpful. On one of those Friday evenings, someone came bursting into the classroom with the news that President Kennedy had been shot. We were stunned but the teacher continued on. I completed the course successfully and signed up to take the exam.

The CPA exam was a three day exam, taken in Columbus, Ohio, and was in four parts: Accounting Theory, Accounting Practice, Business Law and Auditing. Hardly anyone passed all four parts at one sitting, but any part that was passed did not have to be taken over again. So I went to Columbus with one of my classmates, (with my hand on the door handle). I had my dry heaves in the morning and arrived at a building on the Ohio State Fairgrounds. Once inside, I was seated at a small, wobbly, individual desk. I placed my sugar cubes and pocket watch on the desk and was ready to begin. Up front were monitors who were watching us closely to prevent cheating. If any of us had to go to the washroom, a monitor would have to go with us.

As soon as I was back at North American, Mr. Schucard asked me, "How did you do?" I told him that it seemed to go fairly well. All we had to do now was wait for the results. We waited, and waited, and waited some more. I had wanted to pass all four parts on the first try but knew that it would be highly impossible. The results came and I told them to Mr. Schucard - I had passed three parts and only had to retake Auditing which would be a half day exam.

Mr. Schucard was faced with a dilemma. His Assistant Comptroller, Bill Alexander, had taken the CPA exam several times, but had failed. And here I was, well on the road to becoming a CPA. He acted swiftly. He removed Bill's title and regular duties and gave them to me. He sidelined Bill and gave him the title of Cost Accountant and had him just work on cost accounting projects. Bill kept his office with windows which was to the side of the big room. Now I was in charge of preparing the internal consolidated financial statements, working with the outside auditors, doing internal auditing of the plants in various states and the

Canadian subsidiary, handling the annual Internal Revenue Service audit and preparing all of the Corporation Income Tax Returns. I became somewhat of an expert on fireclay percentage depletion and traveled to Washington, D.C., with Mr. Schucard to meet with the Internal Revenue Service and resolve issues on that topic. As you would expect, a large pay raise came with my new position as Assistant Comptroller.

Bill Alexander continued to be friendly towards me, but I could tell that inside, he was quite sad. Bill continued to work at North American Refractories for a couple of years, then he left. I was given his office and had a good view looking out the windows. Later on I learned that Bill had committed suicide and it made me very sad.

I passed the Auditing part of the CPA exam, met the experience requirement based on my internal auditing experience and expertise in fireclay percentage depletion, and became a Certified Public Accountant.

33

A SHIFT IN DIRECTION

enjoyed my work at North American. I enjoyed the accounting, enjoyed the work friendships and enjoyed getting away about once a month to visit one of the plants or fly up to Canada to visit the subsidiary. But as I got to know the Scriptures better, spent time in prayer and meditation and became more comfortable in interacting with people, I began to consider my life's purpose and meaning. At North American I knew that Mr. Schucard was getting close to retirement age and that his position as Comptroller would be open. I also knew that at that time, to qualify as Comptroller I would have to be at least forty years old, which I would not have attained.

Also, at Church, we had a wonderful new pastor, John Walter, who took a personal interest in me. He had several sons and related well to me, so he too became to me like a substitute father. While I was teaching the adult class, he would sit in the back, both listening as I taught, and writing out his sermon notes for the Worship Service that followed. One day, Pastor Walter set me aside and said that he wanted to talk to me. What he had to say was a confirmation of the calling I had been given as a young teen. He said that I should be licensed as a lay minister in the Free Methodist Church and that he would help me in the process. So I took the first step: that of being a licensed exhorter. From time to time I gave a message of encouragement from the Scriptures as the congregation listened. Then Pastor Walter put in my lay minister license application and took me to a District Quarterly Meeting. At the meeting Pastor Walter spoke on my behalf and then I had to stand outside the door while they talked about me. My application was approved and I started the annually required self-study courses to maintain my license. I was now officially a lay minister.

Historians tell us that the early settlers in what is now Ohio built their settlements along the rivers because most of the land was covered with trees and dense vegetation and the rivers provided a fairly easy way to travel and to travel without getting lost. Methodist pastors were very few in number. They would travel up and down the rivers, stopping at each settlement for a while, and then moving on. In between these visits lay ministers did the preaching, teaching, counseling, officiating and met the spiritual needs of the settlers. Initially, my duties as lay minister included some preaching, teaching, visiting the shut-ins and sick, and encouraging people in the Faith.

Also, I felt that I should continue on with my education after graduation from college. However, my personality had changed and I was able to interact better with people, especially one on one, and my speech had improved substantially. After completing all of the required courses in college, one of my elected courses that I took was called "Speech Improvement." In this course a recording of our speech was made at the beginning of the course and also at the end, and we were graded on how much improvement we had made. My grade was an "A." I was now able to speak Northeast American Standard English fairly well.

In considering my life's meaning and purpose, I realized that my accounting career was but a stepping stone to something much greater and more meaningful. At North American I felt that my purpose, other than to meet my and my family's financial needs was to help the wealthy owners become more wealthy. Wouldn't it be better to be a self-supporting minister and in raising my support to be able at the same time to be helping people meet their needs?

So, after twelve years of undergraduate college night classes, earning a BBA degree from Cleveland State University with a major in accounting, I took the law school admission test and enrolled in night law school at Cleveland Marshall College of Law of the Cleveland State University. It was the year 1969.

34

A BIG CHALLENGE

Night law school presented a bigger challenge than I had expected. As I started classes I realized that this was not like the undergraduate startup, like jumping on a moving train, but it was much, much more. It was not the class time but it was the extensive homework, the reading, the preparation to stand up and present an analysis of multiple cases that at first seemed to be overwhelming. I was still somewhat emotionally tired from the twelve years of night classes and needed some time to process many thoughts in my mind. And, of course, my family needed me to spend some time with them. So after two or three weeks of law school, I dropped out.

I did not have any sense of defeat. I still felt led to go to law school. One of my law professors had said that the practice of law and the work of the ministry was a good combination of professions. And I could see that by counseling people on legal matters I could at the same time provide spiritual counseling. Also, my work at North American would provide funds to pay for tuition and books, and having about the same duties every month it would not be that much of a burden. In addition,

I thoroughly enjoyed the thought of studying law. I had studied business law in undergraduate classes and taken it on the CPA exam. I had studied constitutional law for the naturalization process. I had used tax laws at North American and done some tax research for Mr. Schucard. North American owned vast stretches of land in various states and I had worked with issues regarding real property deeds and reviewed business contracts for the Company. So law school was right for me. It was just the timing that was off.

The focus now was on recharging my batteries, on family needs and relationships and on the lay ministry. The month after I dropped out of law school was a month when Arlene, Mike, Beth and I flew over to England and had a wonderful visit with family over there, as I described in a previous chapter. Some of my happiest memories are from that time of my life when I slowed down to a steadier pace. One very precious memory is that of sitting in the Morning Worship service with Beth at my side. She would get weary, lay her head on my lap and go to sleep. That was a regular occurrence.

About that time, I learned a big lesson in communication. Our big old house always needed a lot of maintenance and I liked to do most of the maintenance myself. I especially enjoyed outside painting. There were a lot of children in the neighborhood and Mike and Beth had become friends with many of them. One day, as I was outside, painting the siding at the back of the house, two boys, about eight or nine years old showed up. As they watched me and saw how I was enjoying it they said they wanted to paint too. Realizing that they would likely get white paint on their good clothes, but not wanting to discourage them, I told them that they would need to get their mother to write me a note to say that they were allowed to paint. They left but came back a little while later. To my surprise, they handed me a note from their mother, saying that they were allowed to paint. So I let each of them paint. They each painted for a little while, then were satisfied. Afterward, I thought with horror that maybe their mother thought that we were going to paint pictures at a table. Even today, in counseling couples, I use that experience as an illustration on communication.

I also enjoyed having a small garden. I liked to grow unusual items, like big black radishes and purple beans, which, when cooked, turned green like regular green beans. I grew some giant pumpkins. Arlene and Mike took one on his wagon to Lincoln School only two blocks away to show to the whole class.

The months rolled along, a year had passed, and now I was ready, physically, mentally, emotionally and spiritually for the rigors of law school.

35

LAW SCHOOL NOTES

After a year of anticipation I started back into night law school. Having been a student for two or three weeks the year before, I knew what to expect, or so I thought. But I knew how to pray, and knew that prayer is a two-way conversation, both talking and listening, so I was confident. Being the first year, all of the courses were required courses, starting out with three: introduction to law, contracts and torts. In the introductory course we learned about the court system and general aspects of the law. In contracts we learned about agreements, written, oral and implied. Torts covered everything for which a civil action could be brought that did not arise from contract.

I liked the professor I had in the introductory course. I liked the professor I had for contracts. But the professor I had for torts was quite different. He was a seemingly difficult, hostile man. It was as if he was undergoing personal difficulties and was taking it out on his students. After a few weeks of torts classes I felt, "He doesn't like me. He doesn't like any of us. I can't trust him to grade my work fairly." I knew that to continue in law school I had to have at least a "C" average. So I was impressed to drop torts at that time and take it later with another professor, and so I did. At the end of the semester, all of the grades were posted on the bulletin board. I had done well in my two courses, but when the grades for the torts class were posted, it showed that half of the students in that class had been given "D's" and "F's," meaning that many were unable to continue in law school. I felt so badly for those students who had to leave. Of course, the Law School suffered financially from the loss of all of those students, so the school instituted grading guidelines and made it a rule that professors had to give a percentage range of "A's," a percentage of "B's" and so on to students. But it did not make up for the damages suffered by those who had to leave, to their careers, to them emotionally, financially.........

I continued in law school and completed the first year successfully. It is generally agreed that the first year of law school is the hardest. But then I did something wrong. I had always listened to my Creator God and followed His direction and guidance. For instance, a few years before I had gone down to Columbus for a meeting with the Accounting Board of Ohio, for a hearing on my non-public accounting experience to determine whether it was sufficient for me to be granted the CPA license. After the meeting, I was walking down High Street and intended to eat lunch at a lunch counter in a certain drug store. As I approached the drug store, I felt very strongly that I should not go in. So I went further on and ate at Mills Restaurant. Later on I learned that there had been a shoot-out in the drug store at the time that I would have been in there. I then realized that the very strong feeling that I had had was the Holy Spirit warning me not to go in and keeping me from danger.

The Law School was offering a couple of "easy" elective courses in the summertime. I thought that if I took those courses I would get very high grades and they would boost my grade point average. So I registered, took the courses, got good grades and boosted my grade point average. But I was leaning on my own understanding, getting ahead of the Divine plan, and I suffered for it. That first year had been grueling and I needed a rest. Instead, that summer I was emotionally drained and it was affecting my performance at North American. Mr. Schucard took me aside and told me that my attitude had changed. Thankfully, he was understanding and kept me on. I had learned a lesson, and I got through that difficult time with the help of my forgiving God and with my mother's warning ringing loudly in my ears, "Don't bite off more than you can chew, Brian."

Almost immediately, it was time to enroll in classes again, and as time went on it did seem to go better. The challenge was still great, but I adjusted to the adversarial type of teaching and loved the intellectual stimulation that the study of law offered.

36

HORSEFEATHERS

Besides the intellectual aspect of law school, we were being trained for the adversarial practice of law. Many of us would soon find ourselves in hostile situations. In the courtroom, the Judge may not like us or not like what we would say. Opposing counsel might challenge everything we said or did, and his or her client(s) quite likely would not like us. Even our own client(s) might have higher expectations than what was possible to attain. Or even some or all of these situations would occur simultaneously. How different it would be from the ideal world where people are kind to one another, tender-hearted, forgiving one another and showing love in so many different ways.

So many of the law professors trained us for adversarial practice by ridiculing and challenging whatever we said. Many first year students dropped out within the first few weeks because they could not stand the seemingly endless barrage of criticism. One such professor was the one that I had for Corporation Law. He wore a cape like a Sherlock Holmes outfit. He was a good teacher but he was a terror. One time, he had me stand up for a whole hour on one case we had studied as homework while he asked me question after question about the case. It was like a police interrogation. Thankfully, I had studied well and I was getting a little bit used to the adversarial approach. But each time I would answer a question or make a point he would say, "Horsefeathers, horsefeathers." Now, when I look back and think about that one hour of my life I break out laughing, but at the time it was grueling.

One thing that was lacking in my law school experience, that is very much a part of law practice today, was the lack of teaching of alternative dispute resolution such as mediation and conciliation, encouraging the parties to settle their differences as soon as possible. But I was pleased to open one law book and find a case from the Bible that showed King Solomon's wisdom as a Judge when he was faced with two women, both claiming to be the mother of one baby. King Solomon said, "Cut the baby in half and give half to each woman." The first woman told him to go ahead, but the second woman said to give the baby to the first woman, showing that she was the true mother and did not want her baby to die.

After each week's hostility at the Law School and hard work at North American, I needed a place of refuge, a place where I felt loved and befriended, a place where I was given hope and encouragement. That place, besides being home with the family, was Church. Professor Murad had told our law class, dejectedly, "All we have to look forward to is the grave." I had felt like shouting out, "And the resurrection!" But in those days, I was still plagued somewhat with "British reserve" and was not very expressive of my faith in public.

While I was in night law school, North American Refractories was growing. I developed and installed a profit by product reporting system which was greatly appreciated by management and my staff grew to six people. I was a working supervisor. In those days I was hard on people. I would get after employees for being a few minutes late and not hesitate to fire people who were underperforming. I enjoyed my little office and looked out the window from time to time. One morning I looked out the window at the big United States flag on top of the building across the street. It was a bank building and the flag was being flown upside down - a distress signal. I called the bank and was given assurance that everything was O.K. and they sent a man up to rectify the situation.

North American became a part of Dresser Industries. A year before my graduation, Mr. Schucard retired and Harold Berry became Comptroller. Mr. Berry and I got along reasonably well, but it wasn't the same. Then in January, 1975, I felt that I needed to finish law school that spring by taking some day time classes and concentrate on preparing to take the Bar Exam that summer. So I took a big step of faith. I borrowed five thousand dollars from the bank and gave my two-week notice. My life would be forever changed from that time on.

North American had me come in part-time to train my successor, then I worked part-time for a CPA preparing individual tax returns. I graduated from Law School and was accepted as a candidate to take the Bar Exam. I was thirty-five years old.

37

A CAREER CHANGE

Now came the challenging task of preparing to take the Bar Exam. This would be another three-day exam, also taken in Columbus. This time it would be all or nothing. Those with a score of seventy-five percent or better would pass. Almost all of the candidates would prepare by taking a bar review course. The problem I had was that the review course class times started at nine o'clock in the evening which was definitely not my best time of day. Also, my mind had a habit of going off on a frolic of its own and I thought I might miss a lot of what was being said. So I decided to prepare on my own. I outlined each of the pertinent courses I had taken, then wrote summaries of my outlines. My total focus, apart from the lay ministry, was on passing the Bar Exam. At the church campground, between service times I studied under the big tree in front of the cottage. At home I studied while sitting on the glider on the front porch. On July 4th, 1975, I was studying on the porch when a violent wind came. I could tell that it was no ordinary wind. So I hurried inside and rushed everybody into the basement. Then there was a loud pounding on the side door and a frantic voice yelling, "Let me in!"

We brought a very scared woman into the basement with us. We found out that a large tree limb had come crashing down just as the woman was arriving to visit our neighbors. Later we found out that several people had been killed by falling trees not far from us.

Praying fervently, I took the Bar Exam, with sugar cubes and my pocket watch laying in front of me. Now, I needed to find a position at a law firm so I could support my family and repay the five thousand dollars I had borrowed from the bank. At Christian Business Men's meetings I had met a lawyer by the name of David C. Gibbs, Jr. who had been practicing law for a few years and was now starting a practice with Charles E. Craze, who worked in the steel mill but had recently passed the Bar Exam. Their law office was just a short walk from my house in Lakewood. So I met with David but no commitments were made. My focus shifted to the large law firms in Cleveland and I dropped in on them, one right after another, unannounced. I was able to get several interviews immediately but the response was always the same: they wanted someone younger who they could mold into their way of thinking. At the time that I graduated from law school, there was a glut of new lawyers seeking positions. I did not know yet whether I had passed or failed the Bar Exam, so what should I do?

I went back to David and was able to work out an agreement with David and Charles and began work right away. It was another answer to prayer. Soon, the Bar Exam results were released - I had passed. So now I was able to represent clients and go to court on their behalf. I soon realized that I had made the right choice - it was all part of the Divine plan. I would be able to use all of my training and background in the type of law practice that the three of us now had. For instance, when a person would die, I could handle the legal part, the Probate process, the tax and financial aspects and give grief counseling and relationship counseling to the family, using a combination of all three of my professions. The firm also did a lot of work with churches and Christian ministries. Here again, I was able to use all three of my professions.

Everything went well and about a year after I started, Charles having left the steel mill, we were all working full time in the law practice and all three of us became partners. The law firm's name was Gibbs, Craze and Thompson. We started a Christian First Amendment defense ministry named Christian Law Association. We expanded and moved our offices to Parma Heights, Ohio, where I had a corner office with windows about the full length of two walls. It was great.

38

A GATHERING STORM

S adly, things were not as great at home. Our marital relationship was being affected in many ways. No doubt my heavy schedule with work responsibilities and law school commitments had had some negative impact. After being gone all day I would want to be home. After being home all day Arlene would want to go out. Arlene did start going out a lot, once I arrived home and took over for her. Also, Arlene stopped attending church. So we were together less and less. But it was much more than that. Besides her medical issues, for which she was on hormone medication, Arlene's family history included mental and emotional issues and these seemed to have affected her. One time, after she took a whole lot of pills, I called the local police for assistance. Two officers came immediately, listened for a while, then said, "We're not psychologists," and left.

But my relationships with Mike and Beth were always good. I had always found some time to spend with them. On Sunday afternoons, after my short nap which I always called my "safety valve," we would often go on an organized nature walk in Metroparks then return to the

Nature Center for hot chocolate which we drank while sitting around the fire. Mike and Beth always went with me to church and church camp too. Now that I had completed law school and Beth was a young teenager, I became Young Teen Director at Church and would take Beth and her many friends on social activities: bowling, put put, etc. One of my friends, Ray, was Senior Teen Director and Mike was a senior teen so I would join in many of their activities also. I have many precious memories of all of those times.

Mike, Beth and I encouraged one another during those changing times. Arlene had given some encouragement by giving me a law school graduation celebration with her parents attending. I needed encouragement. The focus in law school at that time was on passing the Bar Exam. It was just about all theory - nothing much on the practical aspects of law practice: the forms, court procedures, etc. All of those had to be learned "on the job." So I would get all worked up whenever I had a new situation such as a hearing in court. Beth was a great blessing to me at such times. I would tell her about the situation I was facing. She would turn to me and say, "You can do it, Dad." My law partners also encouraged me by sharing their experiences. I prayed a lot too but I needed to trust God more and have my faith increased. I had always trusted God and followed His direction in the greater matters of life but I also needed to do the same with the smaller matters.

The law firm was growing and Christian Law Association was growing. Our practice was fast becoming a multi-state law practice as well as a local one. After a somewhat easy start, the work became more and more demanding and there were growing pains. And I had two teenagers at home who needed my guidance and attention, and I needed to spend much time with Arlene. A decision needed to be made. After prayerful consideration I took a gigantic step of faith and dropped out of partnership. My services were still needed by the law firm and I had a good relationship with my former partners, so we were able to work out a part-time work arrangement for me. Also, I gained some clients of my own, including tax clients who I would see once a year at tax time, and through that annual contact I would be able to do their legal work too.

The income would be much less but we were not large spenders and we had enough to meet our needs.

Now I enjoyed the freedom and independence of solo practice. I was able to join several groups including the Gideons with whom I enjoyed distributing New Testaments at the local schools and community college, and the Greater Cleveland Association of Evangelicals in which, over time, I served as officer in several roles. I made many new friends in these groups. I was able to spend more time with clients and give Biblical counseling where applicable. I was able to spend more time with family and in the lay ministry. Arlene and I had marital counseling with the Pastor of the Westlake Free Methodist Church and we seemed to be getting along much better.

I felt that my life was well balanced and that it was in conformity with the Divine plan.

39

DARKENING CLOUDS

I was able to help Mike find his way in life. Mike was not like I was, a reader and writer and counselor. Mike liked to work with his hands. My ability when it came to home repair and maintenance was very limited, but I taught him all that I knew. I had helped with wallpapering as a child and learning to paint was fairly easy. We had one bare wall in the large foyer and I thought that it would be great to cover that entire wall with a mural. So I looked at Sears and found a lifelike wooded scene and we installed it. It was so lifelike that one day our Staffordshire terrier went running right into it and was dumbfounded! We installed ceiling tile and completed a few other projects. Somehow, the woodworking skills of his Grandpa Thompson were passed down to him and he started making furniture. He made a bed frame out of two by fours and proudly used it as his own bed. Encouraging him further, when he was fifteen years old, I let Mike take the car out of the garage, drive it down to the side door and warm the car up. I had paid Mike a small amount for each hour that he helped me on projects around the house, so when he was sixteen he got his driving license and purchased an old Chevrolet.

At age sixteen, with lots of encouragement from Dad, Mike started his own part-time business, "Michael Thompson, Handyman - no job too small." He was successful at it. Sometimes Dad stopped at the job site and helped Mike move furniture. Michael left home at age eighteen and went to live with one of the young men at church.

Somewhere in those years I made a big, big mistake. Arlene had developed a great interest in history, like that of the early settlers and the Civil War. I had a great interest in history as well. So we decided to take some vacation time in Williamsburg and Arlene, especially, was looking forward to the trip with eager anticipation. Just before it was time to go, the dad of one of my former partners needed to have some tax work done and the filing deadline was coming up immediately. Wanting to keep a good relationship with my former partner, I said that I could change my vacation plans and do the tax work. I was thinking that we could just go to Williamsburg at a later date. When I told Arlene, she was devastated. She felt, and rightly so, that I was putting work ahead of her. No forgiveness, but maybe no strong apology, and our relationship went downhill from that time on.

On March 14, 1979, I attended a meeting of the Greater Cleveland Association of Evangelicals. It was held at the Salvation Army facility in the Hough area of Cleveland. It was an enjoyable group of pastors and lay leaders and the program was always enjoyable. We would start by playing volleyball, working up a sweat, then go swimming, then have lunch and a speaker. On this particular day, I left the meeting alone, crossed the parking lot and was ready to get into my new Ford LTD station wagon, when a young man, brandishing a gun, suddenly appeared and said, "This is a raid." I hesitated. The next thing I knew was that I was laying on the ground, my head bleeding and the man was going through my pocket. Then I watched as my station wagon was being driven away. Stunned, I made my way inside, where a "Good Samaritan" got me and took me to Mount Sinai Hospital where the doctor closed up my head wound with a few stitches. That Good Samaritan had been unable to stay, but another Good Samaritan from our group came to the hospital and drove me home. Later on, Dr. Obert removed the stitches without charging me anything for his services.

For a year after I was robbed and pistol-whipped, something was not right. I kept getting flu-like symptoms. The storm was about to hit.

40

THE STORM HITS

At the beginning of May, 1980, the Gideons were having their State Convention in the Greater Cleveland area and I was looking forward to participating in that. But I did not get to go to it. At the end of April I became very ill. Solid foods stayed down and liquids came back up and I did not have any bowel movements. This went on for several days and it reached the situation where I was unable to sit and could hardly move or function. Someone should have taken me to the hospital. On a Friday evening, I managed to take a bath and saw that my abdomen was swollen way out and was hard. Everything was ready to explode. I don't know how I got to the emergency room, but I did. Dr. Obert came to see me and had the head of surgery with him. Dr. Obert wanted my permission to do surgery. I asked him whether it would be like having my appendix removed. He told me how serious my condition was, then I was rushed into surgery.

When I came to, I was in intensive care with a tube down my throat and was hooked up to many monitors and there was a nurse sitting at the bottom corner of my bed, just watching. The ICU that I was in did not have any windows so I could not tell whether it was day or night. This went on for a day or so, then a new crisis hit. Everything started to get dark and I felt that I was dying. Then I was pulling out all of my tubes and seven people were trying to hold me down. I summoned all of my strength and at the top of my voice I preached what I thought was my last sermon, laying out God's plan of salvation through confession, repentance and walking in a manner that pleases Him. Then I felt cool air as doors opened and I was rushed back into surgery. Later I found out that I had acute diverticulitis with blockage, which was followed by perforation and peritonitis. My earlier diet of white bread, cheese sandwiches and soft foods had taken its toll. I was a very sick man.

When I came back from the second surgery, I just lay there, unable to communicate, but I could hear. Mike, pastor friends and Gideon friends came to visit me. I always appreciated it when visitors would speak to me, quote some Scripture or pray, even though I could not respond. After two weeks in intensive care, I was able to eat jello and then was moved into a regular room. After six weeks in the hospital I went home. My body was full of toxins and I was weak and lightheaded. I had a temporary colostomy. I was facing a long period of recovery. Beth helped me by taking short walks with me.

After a while, I was able to do a little work. My former partners graciously loaned me some money to help me get through. I was facing two more surgeries. Dr. Obert kept checking me to see how the two fistulas were healing. Finally, he scheduled me for a six-hour surgery in December to remove scar tissue. Just before I went into Fairview Hospital for that surgery, I received mail from the Court of Common Pleas of Cuyahoga County. Arlene had filed for divorce from me. So I went into surgery with that hanging over my head. My final surgery, to reverse the colostomy, was successfully done in January, 1981.

I was still very weak, sometimes seeing snow in front of me, so I was not in shape to fight the divorce action, nor try to keep the house. My former partner, Charles, represented me in Court. We were divorced in March, after twenty three years of marriage. After the divorce, we would all live together until the house was sold. I had lost my health, was losing my family and about to lose the house I had had for seventeen years.

Dr. Obert was very kind to me. He would only accept as full payment the amount that the basic insurance had paid. I had a supplemental major medical policy with Nationwide and received five thousand dollars from it, but he wanted none of it. I was suffering emotionally and needed to get away for a while. So I took Beth out of school for a few weeks (this was her final year of high school) and she and I flew over to England and stayed with my sister there. That trip was a real blessing and I reached the point where I could walk five miles. I felt that I was on the road to recovery.

41

ON THE ROAD TO RECOVERY

Three months later the house was sold and I moved to a third floor apartment, directly across the street from what had been my house, taking with me a single bed, a recliner chair, my garden spade, small desk and chair, clothing and a few other personal belongings. My bedroom had a window out of which I could see the house. The saddest part was when I watched as my prized piano was being taken away. For two years after that I often dreamed that I returned to the house and the new owners asked what I was doing, being in their house.

But the apartment was perfect for me at that time. My rent was one hundred and seventy five dollars a month including utilities. I was able to do a little work and I had some money from half the equity in the house, so I was able to focus on recovery. I took some continuing education courses and read and memorized a lot of Scripture. In the afternoons I would drive out to the Huntington Reservation of Metroparks and lay on the beach and go into the water, jumping up as the waves came in.

Beth had just graduated from Lakewood High School and went to live with Arlene, and Beth started work at a drug store in downtown Cleveland. So within a short period of time I had lost my health, my family and my house. I also was unable to continue the work of the lay ministry at Cleveland First Free Methodist Church, an inner city church. I had enjoyed the lay ministry there and we had made many friends. I was adult ministries director, Ray was youth ministries director and Dolly was children's ministries director and all three of us were close and completely dedicated to our ministry. Dolly was an unusual person. One summer, the church held a vacation Bible school. Dolly dressed up as a clown and walked around the neighborhood and a lot of children followed her to church.

In my situation, I needed to be ministered to. I transferred my membership and lay minister license to Westlake Free Methodist Church, a suburban church and attended Worship Services there. The pastor's name was Lawrence (Larry) Fryman. At the close of service he would ask me how I was doing. In response I would always quote the Apostle Paul's words, something like "Hard pressed on every side, but not crushed; cast down, but not destroyed." I felt as if I had a big letter "D" stamped on my forehead, but all of the people at the Westlake church welcomed me and encouraged me and that feeling soon went away. While I was with First Church I had written an article entitled, "Come and Help Us" which was published in the denominational magazine called *Light and Life.* One pastor responded to that call and was appointed to First Church, but my lay ministry focus was now to go in a different direction.

A year passed by and my strength was returning although I still had a lot of discomfort from all of the surgeries. I felt ready to start moving on. My target community was now Westlake, Ohio, so I subleased an office in a King James office building in Westlake. The rent was only one hundred dollars a month which was easy for me to pay. The daughter of a Free Methodist pastor friend of mine, Sharon, was attending law school and was in need of a part time position as a law clerk - perfect! I hired her and she was a big blessing. I was working part time at Gibbs & Craze and part time on my own - perfect!

But there was one thing missing. I was lonely. Sometimes Beth came to see me and she had a key to my place. If she came while I was not there she would leave me a note like, "HI Dad Stopped by you not home grabbed a pop & twix have to get groceries home love ya Beth."

Having been married at age eighteen, all I had known was the married life. I longed for companionship and thought about being married again but was unsure about the Biblical aspects of re-marriage after divorce. Arlene had said that she was in love with someone else but I didn't know whether it was all just in her head or not. She had sometimes come home at six o'clock in the morning after being out all night. So I had a counseling session with Pastor Fryman and he reassured me that I could marry again.

Then one day, as I was driving on Clague Road in Westlake, on the way to my office, I was looking at the houses when I suddenly had the feeling that I would have a family and a house again and I was greatly encouraged. I had lunch with one of the women at church and dated one of her friends two or three times. Then I sent away for some profiles from a Christian correspondence organization whose ad I found in the church denominational magazine.

Next, I wrote to Kathy Wolf.

42

A TIME OF NEW BEGINNINGS

Kathy Wolf wrote back to me, then we wrote again and decided to meet in front of a department store, K-Mart in Westlake, and then go out to dinner together. I would wear a yellow jacket so she would recognize me. So we met, had dinner at the Holiday Inn, then we went to a missionary meeting at my church where she met a lot of my friends.

I immediately liked Kathy, and she liked me. It was amazing how much alike we were. She had also been married in Michigan at age eighteen. She and her husband had recently been divorced, and he had remarried. Kathy invited me to her house to meet her four children. She had two teenage daughters, Kim and Teri, and two boys, Donnie age seven and Matt who was almost five years old. We began dating regularly, having supper out together every Saturday and we were often together during the week, especially Friday evenings. I met her parents, George and Rose, who were very friendly and welcoming to me. Rose made an afghan for me to keep me warm in bed and knitted a warm hat and mittens for me. I met Kathy's only sibling, her brother Mike, who was also friendly.

Kathy was a very beautiful woman, and when she smiled her face was radiant. She was not only beautiful in her outward appearance, but she was beautiful on the inside. It was not only her smile, but also her kind, gentle, loving spirit that attracted me to her. We both loved to read, both loved nature, loved to take walks and enjoyed being together. Above all, we both loved to read the Holy Bible and were strong believers. Kathy's children all accepted me, and we became close. I had begun teaching at the Westlake church in the Sunday School hour. So sometimes I would teach class, then drive to the Church of the Nazarene in North Ridgeville and worship with Kathy. My church and her church had the same teachings. So I would sometimes be with Kathy on Sundays as well as Saturday and Friday.

I don't believe that I ever asked Kathy to marry me, but we knew. One day, as I was driving Kathy home, we confirmed it and started making plans. We had dated for a year and built up a strong relationship. She would be my wife and her children would be my children. I had always wanted to have six children and now, to my two, I would instantaneously add four more - perfect! We did not have any formal premarital counseling, but one day we sat on a bench on the west bank of the Rocky River and we decided all of the details of our wedding, honeymoon and life together as a married couple. Kathy would continue to work at the Nazarene daycare for a while. We would sell the house that she jointly owned with her former husband fairly soon, and move to Westlake. We would attend my church in Westlake, and so on.

We had a new pastor in Westlake, Anthony (Tony) Mosely. On August 13, 1983, Kathy and I were married at Westlake Free Methodist Church by Pastor Mosely. The reception was held at Kathy's church, Calvary Ridge Church of the Nazarene in North Ridgeville. Kathy's parents graciously took care of the children while we went on a five day honeymoon trip. We went to Niagara Falls, Ontario, and stopped at Chataqua, New York, and a few other places on the way there and back.

We started our married life together at Kathy's house in North Eaton, Eaton Township, which was in the countryside, and I commuted to work in Westlake and Parma Heights.

A new chapter in my life had begun.

43

A WONDERFUL START

Being married to Kathy was wonderful. It was greater than anything I had envisioned. When we were out together we always held hands. We always kissed hello and goodbye. In my lunch and often amongst my papers I would find little love notes. And we continued to talk together a lot and discuss the Scriptures. She was not only my wife but she was also my best friend. We encouraged one another daily.

I had strong faith, and now I had Kathy's love, encouragement and prayer support which gave me confidence. And I had lost my anxiety. A big question had come into my mind during my time of recovery, "What more could happen to me than has already happened?" And yet I still had strong faith, I had food to eat, my needs were still being supplied and my life had meaning and purpose. Psychotherapists would call it something like "re-interpreting the past in the light of today." So I found freedom from the burden of past difficulties. And I had forgiven Arlene and moved on with my life. Yes, I still had a few butterflies when I was going to speak or have a hearing or do anything new, but it was not any more than what most people would get. I was ready for anything that would come my way.

I found it to be quite different being a step parent rather than a natural parent. I know that my appearance was something of an intrusion on their lives. Kathy took care of the girls and most of their needs while I focused on the boys. They had been living without a dad at home for a few years so their initial attitude was, "You're not my dad, I don't have to listen to you." But that changed rapidly as we interacted and I helped them and showed interest in them, and we quickly became friends. I gave them and Teri rides, took them swimming at the beach, etc. Donnie settled it in his mind by saying that he was lucky to have two dads.

I enjoyed living out in the country. The weekends were quiet and we worshiped at Calvary Ridge. But as the school year was coming to a close, we knew it would soon be time to move. So we engaged a realtor and started looking at available houses in Westlake. We looked at two or three houses, then we looked at a small ranch house on Walter Road. It had three bedrooms and a big family room addition with a separate entrance that would be an ideal place for me to work. We signed an agreement. We applied for a mortgage. Because of my low income years when I had surgeries and was recovering, I realized that there could be some difficulty in qualifying for financing. So I prayed, then I met with the loan officer. She told me that she hesitated to approve our application, but then she got a warm feeling about it and approved us for the mortgage loan. As I left the bank and drove home that day, a double rainbow appeared in the sky. Kathy had a bumper sticker on her van with a picture of a rainbow on it with the words, "God keeps His promises." I felt that the warm feeling that the loan officer had experienced, was from the Holy Spirit answering our prayers.

Moving day came. We all moved in, all six of us. We used every inch of our small house. I realized that the move was hard on the girls. They were leaving their home and community in the quiet countryside and leaving all of the friends they had in school, so I felt for them. And moving day was really sad for Kathy. She had moved into her house with great expectations and this was like the final blow. The boys seemed to think that this was a big adventure with new horizons. I felt assured that this was where I needed to be, just a mile from church and in the needy community I was called to serve.

Kathy, the boys and I would soon adjust. For the girls it would be harder.

44

HAPPILY MARRIED

For the next sixteen years, except for one big tragedy, we were happy; raising the children, working and ministering. Kathy was a very loving, caring wife and mother and also a good cook. She had great insight and often amazed me. Living in the countryside, the boys were used to wandering around wherever they pleased. At first, in Westlake, they did the same thing, crossing peoples' lawns and so on. One day, one of the boys did something wrong. A neighbor living a few doors away, Ron, came rushing to our house, banged on our front door, and said he wanted to beat up their dad. Well, for a few moments I was not their "real" dad and he went away in a huff. Kathy acted quickly. She baked some cookies and had one of the boys take them to him. After that, Ron and the boys became the best of friends. A simple act of kindness had brought peace.

The years went by. The children grew. Kim got married. Teri got married. Our first grandson was born, then our first granddaughter. Soon after we were married, I took Kathy to England to meet my mother and the rest of my family there. This time I rented a car and drove, which proved to be quite a challenge. To drive on the left, sit on the right side of the car, shift with the left hand and drive around those roundabouts and double and triple roundabouts was quite an experience. Then, after getting somewhat used to it, to come back home and drive was another adjustment. We celebrated our wedding anniversary in London. We took many other trips: to Thousand Islands and Montreal, Niagara Falls again, Charleston, West Virginia, and we had many enjoyable picnics. We had a fairly large lot, so I was able to have a large garden and grow fresh vegetables. Kathy loved house plants and had many of them.

My oldest son, Mike, also got married. Two of my sisters came over from England for the wedding and stayed with us for a few weeks. Mike and Therese were a good match. Therese liked to work with her hands too and helped Mike somewhat in his handyman business. They had only been married for a year or two when Mike called me on a Friday night. He could hardly talk, so I knew that something was wrong. He told me that there had been an accident and that Therese had been killed. Not only that, but her mother, her sister and her sister's two little ones had also been killed. What a tragedy. Five were killed in one accident. I went immediately to be with Mike and his father-in-law. We were all stunned. The next day, I helped Mike pick out a casket and make arrangements. Then all five were laid out at the funeral home, the sister with her two little ones laying in the same casket. Then a funeral for all five together. At the funeral, a comforting hymn was sung which had the words, "I will lift you up on eagle's wings." I learned how the accident occurred. The car in which they were riding collided with a truck that was loaded with gravel. Both vehicles went into the ditch. The loaded truck had rolled onto the car. Mike was never the same after that.

After we moved to Westlake, we had a sizeable mortgage payment to make. The interest rate at that time was fourteen and three quarters percent and I had a family to take care of. Soon after moving, the law firm offered me a full-time position. So I took it and closed my office at King James. Kathy left her job at the day care center and took a part-time job at the law firm, doing administrative work, so we often rode to and from work together and had lunch together.

After several years, the law firm decided to move out of the area. I felt led to stay, so I left the firm and started working full-time on my own - a big step of faith - and worked from my office in the home. An amazing thing happened. One wall of my office was almost entirely all window and I looked out into our backyard. Near the office window there was a picnic table out there. Every day, a rabbit would show up at about nine o'clock a.m. and just sit at the corner of the picnic table until late afternoon, then leave. This went on for a few months. I felt that God sent the rabbit to me to keep me company and to assure me that I had done the right thing by leaving the firm and going entirely on my own. God really blessed me that first year. I had two large probate estates and a wrongful death claim to work on, which brought in enough in fees to meet our needs.

There was a new attorney, Patricia Mobberly, who was looking for a part-time position in the legal field. Three different people suggested to her that she should call me. We met and from that time on we practiced law together for some twenty years. She became a good friend of the family. Patricia and her husband lived close by us.

45

ACTIVE IN MINISTRY

During those sixteen years or so, Kathy and I were both active in ministry. When we moved to Westlake, we immediately left Calvary Ridge and became established at the Westlake church, although I did go back and preach twice at Calvary Ridge in their Morning Worship Service. At the Westlake church, Kathy taught the little ones and I taught the adult class. From time to time I preached in the morning worship service. For the people at church, Kathy and I led regular home Bible studies, sometimes in our home and sometimes in the homes of others. The Westlake church held a half hour service at nine o'clock a.m. every Sunday morning at a nursing home, the Welsh Home, in Rocky River. I started to assist there and then soon was leading the service and giving a mini-sermon every week, which I still do today. The law firm had moved downtown, so every week I would attend the Christian Business Men's luncheon and Bible study there and led the Bible study for a year or so. A new retirement facility had been built in Westlake named Club West. I started a Bible study there. I preached at Parkside Church of the Nazarene in Westlake and several times at Trinity

Temple in Cleveland. We regularly attended Family Camp and Kathy's parents both came to faith in Christ there.

In 1999, I had a big challenge. Our pastor at the Westlake church was being assigned elsewhere and a new pastor was to come in. However, at the last minute, we found out that the new pastor was not coming so our church was without any assigned pastor. Being a licensed lay minister and feeling the call of God I stepped forward and served as supply pastor for a year. Kathy helped by typing and running off the weekly bulletins and by doing mailings. I did everything for six months; Welsh Home Service, Sunday Morning Worship Service, including preaching, Sunday Evening Vespers, Wednesday Evening Prayer Service and study and board meetings, etc. Then for the second six months, a retired evangelist, Harold May, came in most weeks to preach in the Morning Worship services. Harold May was amazing. He was eighty three years old but still gave a powerful and effective message. I was basically self-supporting, so I did not have time to do all of the visitation I would have liked to do, but being supply pastor was a wonderful experience.

After those sixteen years, big changes were to take place. Later in the year 2002 I began to experience some impotency and had some discomfort when sitting down. Then later I had some painful sores on my shoulder. Not recognizing what it was, I went to a doctor in Westlake who told me that I had shingles. The doctor also wanted me to have blood work done including a PSA test, so I had that done. The blood work showed that my PSA count was elevated so the doctor referred me to a urologist. Thus began a series of meetings with the urologist during which time my discomfort in sitting increased. I felt as if I were sitting on a coat, with belt buckles and buttons pressing into me. I thought it was my chair. I got a new chair - same thing. The urologist urged me to have a biopsy of my prostate gland done. I finally agreed to it and had the biopsy done.

46

FACING DEATH AGAIN

The urologist called me on my birthday in the evening. We were both home. The urologist wanted us both to get on the line, so Kathy picked up on the extension. He wanted to give us the results of the biopsy. He said that it showed positive and that I had a very aggressive prostate cancer and needed to get in to see him very soon. At his office, he gave me a hormone injection just below my waist and gave me a book about prostate cancer. I read that book from cover to cover and found that it indicated that surgery would be the best option. The urologist referred me to a specialist in another health system who recommended that I have radiation seeds implanted. I met again with the urologist and told him that I wanted to have surgery. He explained to me that because of my prior surgeries it was too risky for me to be opened up from the front and that I would need to be opened from below (perineal), which he was not qualified to do.

A client of mine, who was a medical doctor, referred me to a wonderful urologist, Dr. Kondray, who was qualified and willing to perform a perineal prostatectomy on me. The surgery was done in December of 2003. The surgery showed that my cancer was very aggressive, nine on the Gleason scale, and that the cancer had spread to surrounding tissues. The following month I started a series of thirty nine radiation treatments, and I was to continue on hormone therapy with some chemotherapy for a period that turned out to be about nine years.

I was so glad that I worked from home. Almost immediately after surgery I was able to do some work. I was not able to sit, so I worked standing up for about six hours a day. I believe that being able to work speeded up my recovery from surgery. About seven months after the prostatectomy, I had another surgery, with resulting extreme pain, to install a prosthesis and tubing to overcome impotence. I went on a cancer diet. The hormone therapy with chemotherapy was very hard to take. It gave me continual fatigue, so I had to fight very hard to keep alert and focused. Something in the medication would give me laughing spells, and not just ordinary laughter. I would double over with uncontrollable laughter.

Despite all this I was able to continue to practice law, do tax work and serve as a lay minister. Kathy took a job as a cashier at the garden center which was just around the corner from us and often brought home plants that she had bought there. I enjoyed and took advantage of the family discount at the garden center. We had found a wonderful place for vacation called, "Cottages at the Waters' Edge," which was about four miles west of Vermilion, about a forty minute drive from home, which is where I am writing this chapter today. It is so relaxing to be on the shore of Lake Erie, looking at the beach and the water, watching the blue herons and the occasional bald eagle and other wildlife and watching the beautiful sunsets. This is my fourteenth year here and I am expecting many more.

It is amazing to me how much we can go through and yet survive and even thrive. We prayerfully press on, and God brings us through and our hearts are thankful and full of praise. I had a ten-year battle with a very aggressive cancer, and now I am not on any medications whatsoever and still able to work full-time.

47

A HEART WRENCHING CHANGE

Our twenty-fifth wedding anniversary was coming up in August of 2008. We decided to celebrate by going to Alaska for two weeks. So we flew into Anchorage, stayed in the honeymoon suite at a bed and breakfast there and rented a four-wheel drive SUV. We drove down to Seward and took a day cruise there. We went on a glacier cruise for a day, went for a day to the Alaska state fair, and went to the zoo which had a lot of Alaskan animals. It was amazing. Alaska is so unlike the lower forty-eight. We had a good time.

But our relationship was changing, slowly but drastically. We had signed up for internet service. I used it for business and Kathy for pleasure, but our long conversational time after supper disappeared. Maybe my extra busy year as supply pastor had some effect. No doubt my battle with prostate cancer had some effect. Kathy's religious beliefs changed and her values changed. We no longer discussed the Scriptures together. Then in the year 2010, I sensed that something was really wrong, and then a week before Thanksgiving it all came out. To hear the words, "I had an affair, and it could happen again," is devastating. I knew that I could not continue to live in the situation I was in. Then followed sleepless nights spent pacing the floor, praying for and receiving wisdom and guidance, praying for and receiving coping grace. Papers were filed in the middle of December. On Christmas day I was at Beth's house and she played the song, "Yesterday, all my troubles seemed so far away..." I cried, and cried. Then I went to a family gathering at Kim's house and Kathy was also there.

On New Year's Eve, Kathy and I were home together, just staring at each other. So I invited her out to dinner at Crocker Park, an upscale development in Westlake. After dinner, the New Year's celebration of our sister city, Tralee, in Ireland was shown on a large outdoor screen, with fireworks afterwards. We held hands.

Kathy moved out in January. The divorce hearing was held the week before Valentine's Day. One Saturday, early in the morning, I opened up my desk drawer and there was a picture of Kathy. In the picture she was standing outside the cottage we rented at the lake and she was waving. It was as if she were waving goodbye. I started crying and cried all of that day. I went to a board meeting at church in the late afternoon and cried all through the meeting. For about three months after the divorce Kathy would drop off her two dogs and I would take care of them while she worked at the garden center around the corner. Each time she left we would kiss and embrace. Then she left her job at the garden center.

It was the most difficult time of my life. I had often represented clients in domestic relations court. I had almost always worked towards reconciliation, and many couples had reconciled their differences, and I had only filed for plaintiffs in situations where there were Biblical grounds, which I believe to be adultery and abandonment. But to go through it in my own situation and end a twenty seven year marriage and lose my best earthly friend was extremely hard.

Then came some loneliness. Friday evenings were especially lonely. So I began having special two hour times of prayer on Friday evenings. One time I spent two hours entirely on praise. One time I spend two hours entirely on thanksgiving. In my prayer time I was not alone.

48

A CLOSER WALK

No, I was not alone. God walked beside me. He heard my cry and supplied my need. I learned to totally depend on Him and follow His guidance even in all seemingly little things. When I was cleaning out the house I found some papers and had a three-day battle with bitterness. But during those three days He kept reminding me that we must not let the root of bitterness take hold. So I totally forgave and began to move on with my life. My life has become that of a contemplative and of a servant.

A few months after the divorce, God sent into my life a wonderful Godly woman for three and a half years. We did not spend much time together socially but we continually shared spiritual concerns and blessings, upheld one another in prayer and encouraged one another. Then she decided to marry another friend. It was another adjustment for me. But then He sent yet another Godly woman into my life. She and I do have some companionship times, uphold one another in prayer, encourage one another and do some ministry work together.

That first Christmas as a single, I went to England to visit my four remaining sisters and some of the rest of the family. I stayed with my sister Olive and her husband. Imagine my surprise when I visited the local library to use the internet. I told the ladies there that I was visiting from the United States. One of the ladies replied, saying, "We know, we can tell from your accent." And I grew up in that area!

My first wife, Arlene, had become blind from diabetes and had developed dementia and was confined in a nursing home. After my divorce from Kathy I visited Arlene from time to time. On one of those visits I prayed with her a prayer of confession and repentance. At the end of it she said a loud, "AMEN!" Arlene died a year ago and I officiated at her funeral. I had a lot of good memories to share about our days in East Liverpool. Her body is buried very close to those of my daughter in law and her family.

I see Kathy from time to time at family gatherings. I had prayed about our future relationship and received the word that I should treat her like any other woman, with kindness, gentleness and engage her in small talk, but not contact her outside of family gatherings. So I have followed those instructions carefully.

Mike lives in a tiny cottage on a few wooded acres by the Wayne National Forest in Hocking County, Ohio. Beth still works at a drug store, the successor store chain to the one she started at at age eighteen. Beth is now a Certified Pharmacy Technician and is married. Kim is married and has three children, two girls and a boy. Kim is Fiscal Officer for Carlisle Township and for LaGrange. Teri is married and has three boys. Donnie lives in Texas and is manager at a storage facility. Matt died three years ago at the age of thirty-five. I still have Matt's last text message to me on my hand-held device. I officiated at the wedding of my first grandson, Stephan, and his wife, Samantha, and I go out to eat with them from time to time. All of my children say that they love me and I often get Fathers' Day cards and birthday cards from them.

I've now attained the age of seventy-six and still work full-time as an attorney, CPA and lay minister. My life has meaning and purpose. After my mother died I took Kathy to England for a whole month. We did a lot of sightseeing and visiting. After two and a half weeks, though, I started to feel useless, and though I needed a month away I was glad to get back in the saddle and serve the needs of people again.

I do not plan to retire. I want to continue my life as a contemplative and as a servant as long as I can. I usually wake up singing and sing off and on all day long.

49

I KNOW WHERE
I AM GOING

Sometimes I find myself singing the song that my Uncle Peter would sing as he walked across the kitchen:

"Someday the silver cord will break
And I as now, no more shall sing.
But o' the joy when I awake
Within the palace of the King."

And one benefit of the contemplative life is joy, deep joy, inexpressible joy. To sense the seal of God's approval on our lives, to know that we are diligently following His plan for our lives as He enables us, and to go forward with confidence, knowing that all things work together for good to them that love God, is a wonderful way of life.

As I reflect on my life to this point, I can echo the words of my mother by saying that it's been very hard work, but it's been worth it. I've experienced many blessings in my life and many wonderful relationships with family and friends. Even from what seemed to be the hardest parts of my life I've received many blessings: empathy and understanding toward all who are going through similar situations, a deep appreciation of all who came to my aid and gave me encouragement and prayed for me, and, above all, a closer walk with our Creator God.

A word about how this book came to be written. Last year I was at a church conference meeting when one of the ladies, Zonda Haase, spoke to me and encouraged me to write an article for our denominational magazine about the miracle that happened in my life. I indicated that I would. A few months later I was at the cottage by the lake and prepared to start writing. As I considered the task of writing about the miracle, I thought, "Which miracle - there have been many miracles." It came to me that I should write the whole story, my autobiography. I immediately wrote down the general outline - Divine inspiration. The next eight months I spent bringing up memories of my life's experiences. During that eight month time I was reading Psalm 139 and the title came to me and I realized that the content would be about the way that God has guided me and upheld me throughout all of these seventy six years, which is a theme of that psalm.

God still has a plan for my life. He has given me hope and a future. I will close with an account of one of my recent experiences. This is one of the writings I have had published in a local newspaper.

WHERE ARE WE GOING?

Recently I was in Medina recording an Affidavit. I had to go to three departments in the building, and after I completed the work in the first department, the person there asked me, "Do you know where you are going?" I immediately said, "Third Floor", but then as I turned and headed towards the door, immense joy welled up within me as I pondered that question, and my inner being responded, "Yes, I know where I am going, because I have followed the steps written in the Good News Book, the Holy Bible, and I have assurance of eternal destiny with my Creator."

I know where I am going. As a lay minister I must ask, "do you know where you are going?"

Brian's parents, Wilfred and Florence Thompson, at the time of their wedding

Brian with his older brother, Arthur; his next older sister, Olive; and his younger sister, Grace

Mother Thompson, several of Brian's sisters and two of Brian's nephews at sister Grace's wedding

Brian and his cousin, Mabel

Brian taking a rest while on a long hike in Yorkshire, England

Brian on the Potholing Adventure

Brian at Thornes House Awards Day. Brian is in front row looking down.

Brian's Picture taken by *The Wakefield Express* upon
his completion of the five hundred mile walk

Uncle Peter with his son, Lester and two granddaughters

Graduation Day at Ohio Valley Business College. Brian is in top row third from right. Arlene is in bottom row second from left.

Brian and Arlene at Church campground shortly after marriage.

Brian relaxing on the porch on East Sixty Fifth Street

Arlene standing by our first car, a 1954 Buick Super

Arlene, Mike and Beth on Westminster Bridge in London, England

Brian and grandson, Steve reading while sitting in Brian's favorite chair

Brian's one suitcase after sixty years of wear

One of Brian's recent ventures